VEDANTA

AN ANTHOLOGY OF HINDU SCRIPTURE, COMMENTARY AND POETRY

VEDANTA

AN ANTHOLOGY OF HINDU SCRIPTURE,

COMMENTARY AND POETRY

Edited by Clive Johnson

Under the Supervision of Swami Prabhavananda

HARPER & ROW, PUBLISHERS

New York / Evanston / San Francisco / London

1817

Acknowledgments

APPRECIATIVE ACKNOWLEDGMENTS are made to the following for permission to reprint material included in this book:

ADVAITA ASHRAMA, Mayavati and Calcutta, for selections from *Astavakra Samhita*, Swami Nityaswarupananda, translator, 1969; *Letters of Swami Vivekananda*, 1964; *Complete Works*, Swami Vivekananda, Vol. III, 1960; Vol. IV, 1962.

GEORGE ALLEN & UNWIN LTD., London, for selections from *The Petition To Ram*, Tulsi Das, F. R. Allchin, translator, © 1966 by George Allen & Unwin Ltd.

BHARATIYA VIDYA BHAVAN, Bombay, for selections from *Minstrels of God*, Parts I & II, Bankey Behari, 1956.

DR. V. V. S. KRISHNAMURTHY, Manachanallur, India, for selections from *The Kural or the Maxims of Tiruvalluvar*, translated by V. V. S. Aiyar, 1952.

THE MACMILLAN COMPANY, New York, for selections from *The Hundred Poems of Kabir*, translated by Rabindranath Tagore, assisted by Evelyn Underhill, copyright 1915 by The Macmillan Company, renewed 1953 by Rabindranath Tagore.

G. P. PUTNAM'S SONS, New York, for selections from *Srimad Bhagavatam: The Wisdom of God*, Swami Prabhavananda, translator, copyright 1953 by G. P. Putnam's Sons.

RAMAKRISHNA-VIVEKANANDA CENTER, New York, for selections from *The Gospel of Sri Ramakrishna*, Swami Nikhilananda, translator, 1942; *Inspired Talks, My Master and Other Writings*, Swami Vivekananda, 1939; *Jnana Yoga*, revised edition, Swami Vivekananda, 1955; *The Yogas and Other Works*, Swami Vivekananda, edited by Swami Nikhilananda, 1953.

SHANTI SADAN, London, for selections from *The Ramayana of Valmiki*, Hari Prasad Shastri, translator, 1957.

SRI AUROBINDO ASHRAM, Pondicherry, India, for selections from *Essays on the Gita*, Sri Aurobindo, 1950; *The Life Divine*, Vol. I, Sri Aurobindo, 1939; *The Yoga and Its Objects*, Sri Aurobindo, 1968; *Gems from the Tantras*, M. P. Pandit, 1969.

SRI RAMANASRAMAM, Tiruvannamalai, India, for selections from *Ramana Maharshi and the Path of Self-Knowledge*, Arthur Osborne (published by Samuel Weiser, Inc., New York), 1970; *Talks with Sri Ramana Maharshi*, Sri Ramana Maharshi, fourth edition, 1968.

$\longrightarrow$

FIRST EDITION

LIBRARY OF CONGRESS CATALOG CARD NUMBER: 75-126033

VEDANTA PRESS, Hollywood, for selections from *Vedanta for the Western World*, Christopher Isherwood, editor, 1945; *The Eternal Companion*, Swami Prabhavananda, 1947; *Prayers and Meditations Compiled from the Scriptures of India*, Swami Prabhavananda and Clive Johnson, editors, 1967; *The Upanishads: Breath of the Eternal*, Swami Prabhavananda and Frederick Manchester, translators, 1947; *The Song of God: Bhagavad-Gita*, Swami Prabhavananda and Christopher Isherwood, translators, 1951; *How to Know God: The Yoga Aphorisms of Patanjali*, Swami Prabhavananda and Christopher Isherwood, translators, 1966; *Shankara's Crest-Jewel of Discrimination*, Swami Prabhavananda and Christopher Isherwood, translators, 1947; *The Spiritual Heritage of India*, Swami Prabhavananda (with the assistance of Frederick Manchester), 1964; *Ramakrishna and His Disciples*, Christopher Isherwood, 1965.

To those who search for Truth
whoever and wherever they may be

Contents

V. THE HINDU RENAISSANCE

Foreword

In this anthology we have made selections from the Hindu scriptures, beginning in the era of the prehistoric Vedas and continuing down to the present century. By "scriptures" we mean not only the original holy books, such as the Vedas, the Upanishads and the *Bhagavad-Gita,* but also the sayings and teachings of India's seers and saints throughout the ages. For these seers and saints, like the seers of Vedic times, reached transcendental consciousness, saw and talked with God, and in most cases attained oneness with Him. As teachers they, too, spoke with the authority of direct revelation. Therefore the Hindus accept their teachings as being scriptures also—on the one condition that they do not contradict what is taught in the Vedas and the Upanishads.

But, it may be asked, what essentially *is* this authority of the scriptures? Why should one accept it?

I can best answer this question by describing a conversation I once had with Swami Turiyananda, a direct disciple of Sri Ramakrishna. The swami was a man of God, that is to say he had experienced oneness with Brahman in transcendental consciousness. He was also a great Sanskrit scholar.

At the time when I began studying Shankara's commentary on the *Vedanta Sutras* with the swami, I was a very young man steeped in Western philosophy; I might have been described as a "rationalist." One day I said to him: "Shankara always appeals to the authority of the scriptures to prove his point. But suppose I don't believe in the scriptures? How can he convince me of what he is trying to prove?"

The swami was pleased by this challenging question. He answered: "The authority of the scriptures doesn't depend only on the fact that they are the utterances of great seers; their real authority is that they are verifiable. If these seers had claimed that the truth had been revealed exclusively to them and that it must be accepted from them on trust because it could never again be revealed to anybody else, then your argument would be sound. But what the seers actually say is that these truths can be verified personally by anyone who will follow the instructions given him by his guru and by the scriptures. They also say that one cannot even call oneself spiritual until one has personally experienced these truths."

To quote Shankara: "Erudition, well-articulated speech, a wealth of words, and skill in expounding the scriptures—these things give pleasure to the learned, but they do not bring liberation.

"Study of the scriptures is fruitless as long as Brahman has not been experienced. . . . Therefore those who know the truth should struggle hard to experience Brahman."

Because India has always recognized the supreme importance of direct personal experience of the truth of Brahman, as opposed to passive reliance on the teachings of others, it has continued to produce seers and saints throughout its history. Some of these become known to the world, others remain unknown. As the poet Thomas Gray wrote:

> Full many a gem of purest ray serene
> The dark unfathom'd caves of ocean bear;
> Full many a flower is born to blush unseen,
> And waste its sweetness on the desert air.

In making our selections we have tried throughout to include material of a practical nature; teachings which are timeless and universal and will therefore be of use to any spiritual aspirant—no matter if he is a Christian, a Muslim, a Buddhist, or a Jew.

If the study of this anthology causes even a few students to try earnestly to know the truth of God, we shall consider our effort successful.

—SWAMI PRABHAVANANDA

Hollywood, California

Preface

The spiritual heritage of India is the most ancient known to man—five thousand years is a conservative estimate—and it has given birth to creeds and philosophies of immense diversity. Why, then, have we chosen to title this book *Vedanta*—an apparently limiting term? In one sense, Vedanta does refer to simply the philosophical school of nondualism. But in a larger view, Vedanta means the religion based on the Vedas, the revealed scriptures of India, and the entire body of literature which supports and elaborates them. Vedanta is, therefore, the proper term for Hinduism.

In another sense, Vedanta is a philosophy founded on a set of mystical truths that are in complete agreement with the fundamental teachings of all the great religions. Thus, one can be both a Christian and a Vedantist, for Vedanta accepts and reveres the teachings of the world's great mystics and men of God. Our hope is that we have reflected this attitude in our choice of selections.

Whenever possible, we have avoided the stilted and ponderous translations with their weight of commentary and notes, which so often discourage even the most adventurous from reading them. And with the exception of one or two selections, all of the translations have been made by those steeped in the spiritual heritage of India since their birth.

One of these men is Swami Prabhavananda, my *guru,* for whose guidance I am indeed grateful. He has been an indispensable and affectionate senior partner in this enterprise. His judgment and authority have been called upon time and again throughout the preparation of this manuscript.

My gratitude is also extended to Christopher Isherwood for much valuable editorial advice—and, of course, for his numerous contributions to Vedantic literature; not only as a writer in his own right, but as co-translator with Swami Prabhavananda of many of the basic Hindu scriptures.

I am also deeply grateful to my monastic brother, William Bergfeldt, for his careful reading and typing of the manuscript. His sound advice has been always appreciated. My thanks also go to Nancy Mayorga for preparing the glossary, and for her constant and helpful editorial assistance.

—CLIVE JOHNSON

Ramakrishna Monastery
Trabuco Canyon, California

1. What Is Vedanta?

"Religion is not in doctrines, in dogmas, nor in intellectual argumentation; it is being and becoming. It is realization." In this statement by Swami Vivekananda we find expressed the essence of Vedanta, the eternal religion of India. And, as we shall see, it also suggests why Eastern and Western religious traditions have traveled such widely different paths—and why one day they must meet.

"Knowledge," declared Aldous Huxley, "is a function of being." Man wants to know. The problem of existence, of solving the mystery of who we are and where we are going, has preoccupied thinking persons in every age and culture. Confronted with the inconsistencies of life, its sorrows, and most particularly its failure to bring man any type of lasting happiness, they begin their search for an answer to these questions. Therefore, at the heart of nearly every serious spiritual or philosophical inquiry there exists, often unconsciously, a desire to find some avenue of escape from our own private world of suffering.

What is the cause of such suffering? Man suffers because of a sense of separateness created by the assertion of his own limited selfhood. As a result, he feels alienated from nature, from other men, and from God. Although in the West man has achieved much—scientific advancement, a higher standard of living, triumph over many diseases—within the inner reaches of his own mind he remains largely confused, anxious, and unhappy. And though his "knowledge" has grown enormously, it has failed utterly to bring him any contentment or spiritual security. He has separated himself from the *Tao,* the "Way," and upset the natural order of his life.

A short time ago I came upon an exhibit of books in a nearby public library. In one corner of the display case was a recent history of anesthesia which the author had optimistically titled

1

Triumph Over Pain. If it only were that easy! But it is nonsense to imagine that science has provided a positive cure for pain. We know that physical pain can be endured if we are courageous enough; that it dismisses itself from our consciousness when relief is found. But mental and psychic pains, the sufferings of guilt, anxiety, and spiritual emptiness, can continue for a lifetime. These are life's real pains—and very often its most inarticulate ones. We can say much more easily, "I have a toothache" than "My heart is broken."

It is, again, simply our overconcern with selfhood (with our broken heart) that has created this pernicious suffering. We proclaim this selfhood, though in all innocence, with the severing of the umbilical cord. Thus, through our separation from the source of which we were once a part, we experience our first pain—hunger. With the increasing assertion of individuality, suffering comes to us in subtler guises: as fear, lust, avarice, pride, jealousy, envy, and most of the other all-too-human weaknesses.

It is interesting to observe that when we examine these negative emotions we find in nearly every case their origin to be a positive, pleasurable experience. How is this possible? The answer lies in the fact that intrinsic to every pleasure is its certain termination; a negative reaction—depression, disillusionment, or regret—is inevitable. In Vedanta, these are called the "pairs of opposites"— pleasure and pain, heat and cold, joy and misery, etc. Every action creates a potential and unavoidable reaction. This is essentially what the Vedantist means by *maya*—this pattern of flux, of constant change. Therefore, advises the English poet, "fly the pleasure that bites tomorrow."

Far more profound is a statement by the philosopher Spinoza who recognized, with remarkable insight, the significance of the problem of selfish desire, and that the spiritual problem it poses can be solved only by elevating the mind to a desire for divine things. He wrote in his essay, "On the Improvement of the Understanding":

"For the things which men, to judge by their actions, deem the highest good, are riches, fame, or sensual pleasure. Of these the last is followed by satiety and repentance, the other two are never satiated; the more we have, the more we want; while the love of fame compels us to order our lives by the opinions of others. . . . But if a thing is not loved, no quarrels will arise concerning it, no sadness will be felt if it perishes, no envy if another has it; in short, no disturbances of the mind. All these spring from the love of that which passes away, but the love of a thing eternal and infinite fills the mind wholly with joy, and is unmingled with sadness. Therefore, it is greatly to be desired and to be sought with all our strength."

Nothing in today's world will meet tomorrow's dawn in quite the same condition. Science tells us, for instance, that every seven years the human body undergoes a complete cellular transformation. We become, as it were, "new men." This refusal of phenomenal things to remain static is one of the primary characteristics of physical matter. Therefore, it stands to reason we can expect no consistent pleasure or ultimate happiness from any sense object. It is an unalterable fact of existence. Because of this fact, Vedanta says, the most important goal of the spiritual aspirant is to cease identifying himself with the body, mind, and senses and recognize his true nature, which is divine. Through this supremely creative act, the limiting delusion of selfhood vanishes, suffering ceases, and our souls become united with God. Therefore, the ineluctable duty of religion is to lead man to Self-knowledge, that supreme wisdom through which, as the Gita promises, we "break the contact with pain."

This goal of Self-knowledge is inherent in Indian philosophy, which recognizes no real distinction between the religious and philosophical quest. Philosophical knowledge is identical with spiritual revelation. The closest translation of the word philosophy into Sanskrit is *darshana,* which literally means "seeing" or "experience," referring to the mystical act of divine perception. Unlike Western philosophy, there is nothing speculative or abstract in Indian thought; it is based wholly upon direct and immediate perception of superrational truth. Philosophers are, above all, men of God who have discovered the wisdom of the Self through their own interior searchings. This is the true spirit of Indian religion.

What, then, is Vedanta and its teachings?

In its purest form Vedanta is the philosophy of transcendental knowledge based on the teachings of the Vedas, the ancient, revealed scriptures of the Hindus, as well as the auxiliary teachings and scriptures which have long served to disseminate the truths of the Vedas. In another sense, Vedanta has the figurative meaning of goal or purpose; for literally it means "the end of the Vedas" or the highest goal of wisdom, which is the realization of one's identity with Brahman or God.

At its core, Vedanta is based on three propositions. The first is that the true nature or Self of man (or all intelligent life, for that matter) is God. Second, the purpose of life is to know that this divinity is within us, and realize its identity with the transcendent Godhead. Third, that all religions, though apparently separated by theological differences of creed and various dogmas, are essentially or "mystically" the same.

Let us briefly examine each of these ideas in turn. First we say that man is divine. Such a statement is predicated, of course, on the existence of an infinite and transcendent Being. If this is accepted, then logically such a Being must be all-pervasive. He is therefore within us. To place God in one corner and the world in another imposes contradictions upon both God and the world. For the Vedantist sees the world as not apart from God, but a manifestation of his power and glory. To reject the world as evil and ourselves as sinners is, in a sense, a repudiation of God. Man recognizes good and evil in the world only in the state of ignorance; but the illumined sage, who has transcended ignorance, knows the world to be the house of God. As Swami Brahmananda said: "Show me where matter ends and spirit begins." Only our own private delusion creates separate habitations for God and man.

The Hindus tell a story of a woman ascetic who once visited a particular temple in southern India. Exhausted from a long walk, she decided to rest beneath a tree near the entrance to the temple. As she was resting, one of the priests inside was shocked to observe the woman lying with her feet facing the temple, an act he considered highly disrespectful to the deity. When he pointed out her sacrilege, she replied, "Good sir, please inform me where God is not to be found, and I shall gladly place my feet in that direction."

Second, Vedanta states that the purpose of life is to discover this Self within ourselves and realize its identity with Brahman, the transcendent Godhead. That is to say, the only logical goal in life is the discovery of our true nature, the knowledge of *who we really are.* The majority of men are unhappy and distraught because of their failure to find meaning and purpose in life, because they permit themselves to become identified with their body, mind, and senses.

But aren't we social beings? Not really. For ultimately we are drawn into an awareness that solitude is a basic and inevitable human reality. We come into the world alone, alone we live with our thoughts, and alone we die. Plotinus aptly described the struggle of the spiritual aspirant as the "flight of the alone to the Alone," the solitary struggle of our own mind to penetrate the confusion and disorder we see and feel about us and reach eternal peace. How? Through the practice of meditation, prayer, detachment from sense pleasure, discrimination, and unselfish work. This is the advice of the world's wisest teachers. Thus we can appreciate this ecstatic utterance from the *Taittiriya Upanishad*: "I am life. My glory is like a mountain peak. I am established in the purity of Brahman. I have attained the freedom of Self. I am Brahman, self-luminous, the brightest treasure. I am endowed with wisdom. I am immortal, imperishable."

We now come to the third proposition of Vedanta: that spiritual truth is universal and is found at the heart of all religions. "A common man, through ignorance," said Sri Ramakrishna, the nineteenth-century saint, "considers his own religion to be the best and makes much clamor. But when his mind is illumined by knowledge, all such quarreling disappears." Mystical knowledge at once grants us insight into the essential nature of religion, for true religion is founded upon revelation, not the inventions or speculations of men. Vedantists refer to this essential or enduring aspect of religion as the *sanatana dharma* or eternal path, which is ever-abiding and ageless. The various religions are merely the external expressions of this path—vehicles required by man in his journey to Truth. The *Bhagavad-Gita,* the first scripture to stress the harmony of the various pathways to God, states through the lips of Sri Krishna:

> Whatever path men travel
> Is my path:
> No matter where they walk
> It leads to me.

Religious disputes inevitably arise as the result of various differences in race, culture, society, temperament and so forth. No religion is totally free from prejudice or feelings of exclusiveness. At the same time, Vedanta makes a sharp distinction between the external and internal nature of religion; it urges us to look beyond the differences in order to realize the unity of all faiths, for the highest manifestation of God is found within man—that eternal and unwavering Self, which is beyond dogma or doctrine. In man himself lies the supreme unity, and it is there he must begin—and end—his search. This is the message of Vedanta.

C. J.

I

THE REVEALED SCRIPTURES

2. The Vedas

The Vedas occupy a singular place in the religion of India. Not only are they the oldest scriptures of the world, but they are also considered by orthodox Hindus to be their most important. They are the cornerstone of Hinduism. Even to call them the oldest is somewhat deceptive, for the Vedas are accepted as eternal truths. In ancient times, they were transmitted orally from teacher to disciple; only in later centuries were they committed to writing. For this reason, no real dates can be assigned to them. The Vedas belong to that category of scriptures known as *shruti* (from the Sanskrit *shru,* to hear) or teachings which were revealed to the ancient sages while in communion with God.

One rather remarkable characteristic of the Vedas is that they depend on no external authority for their proof. They themselves *are* the authority, and any spiritual aspirant can verify their truth for himself in transcendental consciousness.

There are four Vedas: the *Rik, Sama, Yajus,* and *Atharva.**
These are divided into two categories: the Work Portion and the Knowledge Portion. The Work Portion includes the *Samhitas* or hymns (*mantras*), which generally praise various deities; the *Brahmanas* or rules of conduct and performance of rites; and the *Aranyakas* or forest treatises, which concern themselves with symbolic rites and ceremonies. The Knowledge Portion consists of the Upanishads, which will be treated in the next section. Together, these two serve as the basis of all the other Hindu scriptures.

The Vedas mention many gods and goddesses, a fact which almost at once prompts the Westerner (including many scholars) to think of Hinduism as elaborately polytheistic. Although it is true that the Hindu has many gods, it should be recognized that

* Spellings differ slightly when joined with the word "Veda."

9

these various deities are only so many manifestations of the same Godhead. In the *Rig Veda,* the most ancient of Hindu scriptures, we find this statement: "Truth is one; sages call it by various names." Hinduism appeals to all classes of people and degrees of spiritual development. For some the concept of a personal God is necessary; others might be drawn to only the formless, impersonal Brahman. For instance, in the selections to follow we find one of the loftiest poems ever written, the "Hymn to Creation," totally impersonal. Another, more intimate in tone, is a prayer for protection and health. Such diversity, however, ultimately resolves itself into a central oneness that forms the underlying spirit of Hinduism. We shall find that this mystical theme of unity in variety characterizes nearly all the other Vedantic scriptures as well.

The Vedas

PEACE CHANT

May my speech be one with my mind, and may my mind be one with my speech.
O thou self-luminous Brahman, remove the veil of ignorance from before me, that I may behold thy light.
Do thou reveal to me the spirit of the scriptures.
May the truth of the scriptures be ever present to me.
May I seek day and night to realize what I learn from the sages.
May I speak the truth of Brahman.
May I speak the truth.
May it protect me.
May it protect my teacher.
            OM . . . Peace—peace—peace.[1]

                                        [*Rig Veda*]

GAYATRI MANTRA

May we meditate on the effulgent Light of him who is worshipful, and who has given birth to all worlds. May he direct the rays of our intelligence towards the path of good.

                                        [*Rig Veda*]

THE HYMN OF CREATION

Existence was not, nor its opposite,
Nor earth, nor heaven's blue vault, nor aught beyond.
The subtle elements that are the veil
Of this so insubstantial world, where then
Might they find out a place? By whom be known?
The deep abyss of waters—where was that?

Death was not yet, nor deathlessness; the day
Was night, night day, for neither day nor night
Had come to birth. Then THAT, the primal fount
Of life—breathless—to its own maya joined—
Brooded eternally. Itself beside,
In the wide universe there nothing was.

In the beginning gloom—gloom hidden in gloom!
From its cause undistinguished stood the world:
But lo, thereafter, from its darkling state—
Yet undistinguished from its cause—it rose,
By the pure will of THAT made manifest.

Whence came this will? From out a seed it came
Asleep within the heart of THAT—the seed
Of vanished worlds that have in order wheeled
Their silent courses from eternity:
The manifest in the unmanifest they found—
The sages, searching deep within themselves.

As from the rising sun the beams spread forth
In sudden splendor, and no man can tell
Which first, which in the midst, which last—so came
The universe from THAT. Twofold it was,
Subject and object—subject, to enjoy;
Object, to be enjoyed: and of these twain
The first is higher in creation's scale.

Ah, what are words, and what all mortal thought!
Who is there truly knows, and who can say,
Whence this unfathomed world, and from what cause?

Nay, even the gods were not! Who, then, can know?
The source from which this universe hath sprung,
That source, and that alone, which bears it up—
None else: THAT, THAT alone, lord of the worlds,
In its own self contained, immaculate
As are the heavens above, THAT alone knows
The truth of what itself hath made—none else!

[*Rig Veda,* X. 121. 1-7]

THE UNIVERSAL BEING

The Universal Being has infinite heads, unnumbered eyes, and
unnumbered feet.
Enveloping the universe on every side, he exists transcending it.
All this is he—what has been and what shall be.
He is the lord of immortality.
Though he has become all this, in reality he is not all this:
For verily is he transcendental.
The whole series of universes—past, present, and future—express
his glory and power;
But he transcends his own glory.
All beings of the universe form, as it were, a fraction of his being;
The rest of it is self-luminous, and unchangeable.
He who is beyond all predicates exists as the relative universe.
That part of him which is the relative universe appears as sen-
tient and insentient beings.
From a part of him was born the body of the universe, and out
of this body were born the gods, the earth, and man.

[*Rig Veda,* X. 90. 1-5]

HYMN TO VARUNA*

Wherever two together plot, and deem they are alone,
King Varuna is there, a third, and all their schemes are known.
This earth is his, to him belong these vast and boundless skies;

* Varuna is god of the sky. But as represented in this hymn, he is con-
ceived of as the controller of the moral order of the universe, the Supreme
Being within which the physical world is contained.

Both seas within him rest, and yet in that small pool he lies.
Whoever far beyond the sky should think his way to wing,
He could not there elude the grasp of Varuna the king.
His spies descending from the skies glide all this world around;
Their thousand eyes all-scanning sweep to earth's remotest bound.
Whate'er exists in heaven and earth, whate'er beyond the skies,
Before the eyes of Varuna, the king, unfolded lies.
The ceaseless winkings all he counts of every mortal's eyes:
He wields this universal frame, as gamester throws his dice.[2]

[Atharva Veda, IV. 16. 1-5]

PRAYER FOR THE ATTAINMENT OF THE KNOWLEDGE OF BRAHMAN

I take refuge in thee, O Lord.
Thou dost deliver man from the bondage of birth and rebirth.
I bow down to thee.
Lead me not into the wheel of birth and rebirth, but guide me over
    to the shore of immortality.
My obeisance to thee.
I bow down to thee, O Lord.
Thou art the Ancient One. I bow down to thee.
Thou art supreme. I bow down to thee.
Thou art mighty. I bow down to thee.
Thou art time. I bow down to thee.
Thou art the Word that is in the beginning. I bow down to thee.
Thou art the source of strength. I bow down to thee.
Thou art the subduer of the tyrant. I bow down to thee.
Thou art the ruler of all beings. I bow down to thee.
Thou art the ruler of the mind. I bow down to thee.[3]

[Yajur Veda, Taitt. Aranyaka, x. 43-47]

PRAYER FOR THE REMOVAL OF OBSTACLES TO KNOWLEDGE

May the truth of Brahman be revealed unto me.
May the Supreme Joy be realized by me.
May Brahman who is Supreme Joy be revealed unto me.

O thou, the Supreme Self, thou bestowest the knowledge of Brahman.

I am one of thy creatures.

I am thy servant.

I am thy child.

Assuredly, I am worthy of thy grace.

O thou, destroyer of this evil dream of a world, remove all my sufferings forever.

O thou, Supreme Self, bestower of the knowledge of Brahman, it is to thee, in truth, that my senses, my vital forces and my mind belong.

May I offer them unto thee.

May they be withdrawn from all external objects and absorbed in thee.

May I have whole-souled devotion to thee.

May I attain Brahman through right understanding.

May I attain the Supreme Joy through right understanding.

May I attain Brahman, the Supreme Joy, through right understanding, which enables one to grasp the truth of the great saying, as it is imparted by the guru.

O Inspirer of right understanding, grant us, who are spiritual aspirants, the good fortune to become illumined teachers with many disciples and followers.

Remove our evil dream of duality.

Wipe out all sins that obstruct the path to right knowledge.

Grant us that knowledge of the Truth which is beyond all doubts and misconceptions.

May the winds blow sweetly,

May the rivers flow sweetly,

May plants and herbs be sweet to us,

May days and nights be sweet to us,

May the dust of the earth be sweet to us,

May the heaven that protects us be sweet to us,

May the trees be sweet to us,

May the sun shine on us sweetly,

May the cows yield us sweet milk.

Selfless service leads to the knowledge of Brahman.

Selfless service leads to the Supreme Joy.

Selfless service leads to Brahman, the Supreme Joy.
Among gods, Brahman is the four-faced Brahma;
Among poets, He is the one who is known as the greatest;
Among the seekers of truth, He is the seer;
Among the beasts, He is the buffalo;
Among birds, He is the eagle;
In the woods, He is the axe
In a sacrificial rite, He is the sacred soma, sanctified by the
sacred mantra.

[*Yajur Veda, Taitt. Aranyaka,* x. 48-50]

PRAYER FOR RIGHT UNDERSTANDING

We offer our adoration to Thee, O Goddess of understanding.
Be favorable unto us.
Be gracious unto us.
Be Thou ever beneficent.
Mayest Thou reveal unto us the innermost of all truths!
Even if perchance we be engaged in actions and thoughts not
enjoined by the scriptures and inimical to realization of the
Supreme Goal,
Withhold not Thy grace.
Being favored by Thee, may we remain true to the spiritual ideals
taught by the Vedas.
May we, as worthy disciples, perform selfless actions, and, thus
purified, may we dwell in the Supreme Brahman.

By Thy grace, O Mother, a man can attain the knowledge of
Brahman;
Or he can gain the position of Brahma;
Or he can find glory, or win untold riches.
Favor us with well-being, O Goddess.

May Indra grant me right understanding.
May the Goddess of Wisdom grant me right understanding.
May the twin gods garlanded with lotus flowers grant me right
understanding.
The right understanding that is in the celestial maidens,
The right understanding possessed by the heavenly singers,

The right understanding that belongs to the great gods,
The right understanding that is in the knowers of the Vedic lore;
May that right understanding dwell in me, and make my life
sweet and fragrant.

[*Yajur Veda, Taitt. Aranyaka*, x. 39-42]

NOTES

1. This selection and those following translated by Swami Prabhavananda and Frederick Manchester in Swami Prabhavananda, *The Spiritual Heritage of India* (1964), unless otherwise noted.

2. Translated by John Muir.

3. This prayer and those following translated by Swami Prabhavananda and Swami Satprakashananda in Swami Prabhavananda and Clive Johnson, editors, *Prayers and Meditations Compiled from the Scriptures of India* (1967). (They originally appeared in *Vedanta and the West* magazine number 105.)

3. The Upanishads

The word *upanishad* literally means "sitting near devotedly," which immediately brings to mind a disciple eagerly absorbing the teachings of his spiritual master or *guru*. This directness is a dominant characteristic of the Upanishads, for the Hindu believes the highest and noblest truths are learned from the lips of an enlightened teacher.

The Upanishads, as part of the Vedas, express eternal truths; in a sense, then, they cannot be related to any specific period in time nor to any known author. We do not even know how many Upanishads were written, although 108 have been preserved. Of these, sixteen were considered particularly important treatises by Shankara, the eighth-century philosopher and sage, who wrote commentaries on ten of them. These have come to be known as the principal Upanishads. They are: *Isha, Kena, Katha, Prashna, Mundaka, Mandukya, Aitareya, Taittiriya, Chandogya,* and *Brihadaranyaka.*

Though apparently quite diverse, the Upanishads have a number of characteristics in common. First, there is a basic homogeneity of meaning and purpose. Despite differences in philosophical approach and literary technique, the treatises echo one another in the acceptance of Brahman as the only Reality and the world as transitory or unreal. When the Hindu speaks of the world as unreal he means it in this sense: that it is ever-changing. It exists, certainly; but it has no permanent reality. Only Brahman or God is immutable.

A second characteristic is that they all emphasize the identity of the Impersonal Brahman with the Atman, the indwelling Self or Godhead in all creatures. We find this expressed in the famous statement *Tat Tvam asi*—"That Thou art." The purpose of life, the Upanishads tell us, is to realize this unity by transcending the three states of ordinary consciousness—waking, dreaming, and dreamless sleep. Prajapati's teaching in the *Chandogya Upanishad,* for example, vividly illustrates this identity of Atman and Brahman.

Still another characteristic is that all of the Upanishads were communicated by illumined saints whose only purpose was to enlighten others and thereby relieve the suffering of mankind. Their task was not to create philosophical schools or systems, but to record for posterity the truth of their inner experience.

The Upanishads

Isha

In the heart of all things, of whatever there is in the universe, dwells the Lord. He alone is the reality. Wherefore, renouncing vain appearances, rejoice in him. Covet no man's wealth.

Well may he be content to live a hundred years who acts without attachment—who works his work with earnestness, but without desire, not yearning for its fruits—he, and he alone.

Worlds there are without suns, covered up with darkness. To these after death go the ignorant, slayers of the Self.*

The Self is one. Unmoving, it moves swifter than thought. The senses do not overtake it, for always it goes before. Remaining still, it outstrips all that run. Without the Self, there is no life. . . .

He who sees all beings in the Self, and the Self in all beings, hates none.

To the illumined soul, the Self is all. For him who sees everywhere oneness, how can there be delusion or grief?

The Self is everywhere. Bright is he, bodiless, without scar of imperfection, without bone, without flesh, pure, untouched by evil. The Seer, the Thinker, the One who is above all, the Self-Existent—he it is that has established perfect order among objects and beings from beginningless time.

[1-4; 6-8]

* The Atman or Inner Being. Atman is identical with Brahman.

Kena

At whose behest does the mind think? Who bids the body live? Who makes the tongue speak? Who is that effulgent Being that directs the eye to form and color and the ear to sound?

The Self is ear of the ear, mind of the mind, speech of the speech. He is also breath of the breath, and eye of the eye. Having given up the false identification of the Self with the senses and the mind, and knowing the Self to be Brahman, the wise, on departing this world, become immortal.

Him the eye does not see, nor the tongue express, nor the mind grasp. Him we neither know nor are able to teach. Different is he from the known, and different is he from the unknown. So have we heard from the wise.

[I. 1-4]

Katha

On a certain occasion Vajasrabasa, hoping for divine favor, performed a rite which required that he should give away all his possessions. He was careful, however, to sacrifice only his cattle, and of these only such as were useless—the old, the barren, the blind, and the lame. Observing this niggardliness, Nachiketa, his young son, whose heart had received the truth taught in the scriptures, thought to himself: "Surely a worshiper who dares bring such worthless gifts is doomed to utter darkness!" Thus reflecting, he came to his father, and cried:

"Father, I too belong to thee: to whom givest thou *me?*"

His father did not answer; but when Nachiketa asked the question again and yet again, he replied impatiently:

"Thee I give to Death!"

. . . being determined to keep his father's word [Nachiketa] said: "Father, do not repent thy vow! Consider how it has been with those that have gone before, and how it will be with those that now live. Like corn, a man ripens and falls to the ground; like corn, he springs up again in his season."

Having thus spoken, the boy journeyed to the house of Death. But the god was not at home, and for three nights Nachiketa waited. When at length the King of Death returned, he was met by his servants, who said to him:

"A Brahmin, like to a flame of fire, entered thy house as guest, and thou wast not there. Therefore must a peace offering be made to him. . . ."

Then the King of Death approached Nachiketa and welcomed him with courteous words.

"O Brahmin," he said, "I salute thee. Thou art indeed a guest worthy of all reverence. Let, I pray thee, no harm befall me! Three nights hast thou passed in my house and hast not received my hospitality; ask of me, therefore, three boons—one for each night."

[I. i. 1-9]

[*For his first boon, Nachiketa asks Yama to appease the anger of his father and permit him to be welcomed home with love. This Yama readily grants. His second boon is for knowledge of the fire sacrifice by which one gains the joy and peace of heaven. This also is granted him. Then Nachiketa asks his third boon.*—Ed.]

"When a man dies, there is this doubt: some say, he is; others say, he is not. Taught by thee, I would know the truth. This is my third wish."

"Nay," replied Death, "even the gods were once puzzled by this mystery. Subtle indeed is the truth regarding it, not easy to understand. Choose thou some other boon, O Nachiketa."

But Nachiketa would not be denied.

"Thou sayest, O Death, that even the gods were once puzzled by this mystery, and that it is not easy to understand. Surely there is no teacher better able to explain it than thou—and there is no other boon equal to this."

To which, trying Nachiketa again, the god replied:

"Ask for sons and grandsons who shall live a hundred years. Ask for cattle, elephants, horses, gold. Choose for thyself a mighty kingdom. Or if thou canst imagine aught better, ask for that— not for sweet pleasures only but for the power, beyond all thought, to taste their sweetness. Yea, verily, the supreme enjoyer will I make thee of every good thing. Celestial maidens, beautiful to behold, such indeed as were not meant for mortals—even these, together with their bright chariots and their musical instruments, will I give unto thee, to serve thee. But for the secret of death, O Nachiketa, do not ask!"

But Nachiketa stood fast, and said: "These things endure only till the morrow, O Destroyer of Life, and the pleasures they give wear out the senses. Keep thou therefore horses and chariots, keep dance and song, for thyself! How shall he desire wealth, O Death, who once has seen thy face? Nay, only the boon that I have chosen—that only do I ask. Having found out the society of the imperishable and the immortal, as in knowing thee I have done, how shall I, subject to decay and death, and knowing well the vanity of the flesh—how shall I wish for long life?

"Tell me, O King, the supreme secret regarding which men doubt. No other boon will I ask."

Whereupon the King of Death, well pleased at heart, began to teach Nachiketa the secret of immortality.

[I. i. 20-29]

King of Death

The good is one thing; the pleasant is another. These two, differing in their ends, both prompt to action. Blessed are they that choose the good; they that choose the pleasant miss the goal.

Both the good and the pleasant present themselves to men. The wise, having examined both, distinguish the one from the other. The wise prefer the good to the pleasant; the foolish, driven by fleshly desires, prefer the pleasant to the good. . . .

Thou, O Nachiketa, having looked upon fleshly desires, delightful to the senses, hast renounced them all. Thou hast turned from the miry way wherein many a man wallows.

Far from each other, and leading to different ends, are ignorance and knowledge. Thee, O Nachiketa, I regard as one who aspires after knowledge, for a multitude of pleasant objects were unable to tempt thee. . . .

The truth of the Self cannot be fully understood when taught by an ignorant man, for opinions regarding it, not founded in knowledge, vary one from another. Subtler than the subtlest is this Self, and beyond all logic. Taught by a teacher who knows the Self and Brahman as one, a man leaves vain theory behind and attains to truth. . . .

Smaller than the smallest, greater than the greatest, this Self forever dwells within the hearts of all. When a man is free from desire, his mind and senses purified, he beholds the glory of the Self and is without sorrow.

Though seated, he travels far; though at rest, he moves all things. Who but the purest of the pure can realize this Effulgent Being, who is joy and who is beyond joy.

Formless is he, though inhabiting form. In the midst of the fleeting he abides forever. All-pervading and supreme is the Self. The wise man, knowing him in his true nature, transcends all grief.

The self is not known through study of the scriptures, nor through subtlety of the intellect, nor through much learning. But by him who longs for him is he known. Verily unto him does the Self reveal his true being.

By learning a man cannot know him, if he desist not from evil, if he control not his senses, if he quiet not his mind, and practice not meditation.

[I. ii. 1-4; 8; 20-24]

Know that the Self is the rider, and the body the chariot; that the intellect is the charioteer, and the mind the reins.*

The senses, say the wise, are the horses; the roads they travel are the mazes of desire. The wise call the Self the enjoyer when he is united with the body, the senses, and the mind.

When a man lacks discrimination and his mind is uncontrolled, his senses are unmanageable, like the restive horses of a charioteer. But when a man has discrimination and his mind is controlled, his senses, like the well-broken horses of a charioteer, lightly obey the rein.

He who lacks discrimination, whose mind is unsteady and whose heart is impure, never reaches the goal, but is born again and again. But he who has discrimination, whose mind is steady and

* According to Hindu psychology, the mind-stuff (chitta) has three components: manas or that which receives sense impressions; buddhi or the intellect that receives these impressions and performs the function of discrimination; and ahamkara or the ego-sense, which claims these impressions for itself and creates the feeling of individuality. Mind, as used in the above paragraph, refers to its function as an organ of perception (manas).

whose heart is pure, reaches the goal, and having reached it is born no more.

The man who has a sound understanding for charioteer, a controlled mind for reins—he it is that reaches the end of the journey, the supreme abode of Vishnu, the all-pervading.*. . .

Brahman is the end of the journey. Brahman is the supreme goal. This Brahman, this Self deep-hidden in all things, is not revealed to all; but to the seers, pure in heart, concentrated in mind—to them is he revealed.

The senses of the wise man obey his mind, his mind obeys his intellect, his intellect obeys his ego, and his ego obeys the Self.

Arise! Awake! Approach the feet of the Master and know THAT. Like the sharp edge of a razor, the sages say, is the path. Narrow it is, and difficult to tread!

Soundless, formless, intangible, undying, tasteless, odorless, eternal, without beginning, without end, immutable, beyond nature, is the Self. Knowing him as such, one is freed from death. . . .

The Self-Existent made the senses turn outward. Accordingly, man looks toward what is without, and sees not what is within. Rare is he who, longing for immortality, shuts his eyes to what is without and beholds the Self.

[I. iii. 3-9; 12-15; II. i. 1]

He, the adorable one, seated in the heart, is the power that gives breath. Unto him all the senses do homage.

What can remain when the dweller in this body leaves the outgrown shell, since he is, verily, the immortal Self?

Man does not live by breath alone, but by him in whom is the power of breath. . . .

As the sun, revealer of all objects to the seer, is not harmed by the sinful eye, nor by the impurities of the objects it gazes on, so the one Self, dwelling in all, is not touched by the evils of the world. For he transcends all.

He is one, the lord and innermost Self of all; of one form, he makes of himself many forms. To him who sees the Self re-

* Vishnu is equivalent here to Brahman.

vealed in his own heart belongs eternal bliss—to none else, to none else! . . .

[II. ii. 3-5; 11-12]

None beholds him with the eyes, for he is without visible form. Yet in the heart is he revealed, through self-control and meditation. Those who know him become immortal.

When all the senses are stilled, when the mind is at rest, when the intellect wavers not—that, say the wise, is the highest state.

This calm of the senses and the mind has been defined as yoga. He who attains it is freed from delusion. . . .

The Supreme Person, of the size of a thumb, the innermost Self, dwells forever in the hearts of all beings. As one draws the pith from a reed, so must the aspirant after truth, with great perseverance, separate the Self from the body. Know the Self to be pure and immortal—yea, pure and immortal!

[II. iii. 9-11; 17]

Mundaka

Self-luminous is Brahman, ever present in the hearts of all. He is the refuge of all, he is the supreme goal. In him exists all that moves and breathes. In him exists all that is. He is both that which is gross and that which is subtle. Adorable is he. Beyond the ken of the senses is he. Supreme is he. Attain thou him! . . .

Affix to the Upanishad, the bow incomparable, the sharp arrow of devotional worship; then, with mind absorbed and heart melted in love, draw the arrow and hit the mark—the imperishable Brahman.

OM is the bow, the arrow is the individual being, and Brahman is the target. With a tranquil heart, take aim. Lose thyself in him, even as the arrow is lost in the target.

In him are woven heaven, earth, and sky, together with the mind and all the senses. Know him, the Self alone. Give up vain talk. He is the bridge of immortality.

Within the lotus of the heart he dwells, where, like the spokes of a wheel, the nerves meet. Meditate on him as OM. Easily mayest thou cross the sea of darkness.

This Self, who understands all, who knows all, and whose glory is manifest in the universe, lives within the lotus of the heart, the bright throne of Brahman. By the pure in heart is he known. The Self exists in man, within the lotus of the heart, and is the master of his life and of his body. With mind illumined by the power of meditation, the wise know him, the blissful, the immortal.

The knot of ignorance of the heart is loosed, all doubts are dissolved, all evil effects of deeds are destroyed, when he who is both personal and impersonal is realized.

In the effulgent lotus of the heart dwells Brahman, who is passionless and indivisible. He is pure, he is the light of lights. Him the knowers of the Self attain.

Him the sun does not illumine, nor the moon, nor the stars, nor the lightning—nor, verily, fires kindled upon earth. He is the one light that gives light to all. He shining, everything shines.

This immortal Brahman is before, this immortal Brahman is behind, this immortal Brahman extends to the right and to the left, above and below. Verily, all is Brahman, and Brahman is supreme.

[II. ii. 1-2; 3-11]

Like two birds of golden plumage, inseparable companions, the individual self and the immortal Self are perched on the branches of the selfsame tree. The former tastes of the sweet and bitter fruits of the tree; the latter, tasting of neither, calmly observes.

The individual self, deluded by forgetfulness of his identity with the divine Self, bewildered by his ego, grieves and is sad. But when he recognizes the worshipful Lord as his own true Self, and beholds his glory, he grieves no more.

When the seer beholds the Effulgent One, the Lord, the Supreme Being, then, transcending both good and evil, and freed from impurities, he unites himself with him.

The Lord is the one life shining forth from every creature. Seeing him present in all, the wise man is humble, puts not himself forward. His delight is in the Self, his joy is in the Self, he serves the Lord in all. Such as he, indeed, are the true knowers of Brahman.

This Effulgent Self is to be realized within the lotus of the heart by continence, by steadfastness in truth and meditation, and by superconscious vision. Their impurities washed away, the seers realize him.

Truth alone succeeds, not untruth. By truthfulness the path of felicity is opened up, the path which is taken by the sages, freed from cravings, and which leads them to truth's eternal abode.

Brahman is supreme; he is self-luminous, he is beyond all thought. Subtler than the subtlest is he, farther than the farthest, nearer than the nearest. He resides in the lotus of the heart of every being.

The eyes do not see him, speech cannot utter him, the senses cannot reach him. He is to be attained neither by austerity nor by sacrificial rites. When through discrimination the heart has become pure, then, in meditation, the Impersonal Self is revealed.

The subtle Self within the living and breathing body is realized in that pure consciousness wherein is no duality—that consciousness by which the heart beats and the senses perform their office.

Whether of heaven, or of heavenly enjoyments, whether of desires, or of objects of desire, whatever thought arises in the heart of the sage is fulfilled. Therefore let him who seeks his own good revere and worship the sage.

[III. i.]

The sage knows Brahman, the support of all, the pure effulgent being in whom is contained the universe. They who worship the sage, and do so without thought of self, cross the boundary of birth and death.

He who, brooding upon sense objects, comes to yearn for them, is born here and there, again and again, driven by his desire. But he who has realized the Self, and thus satisfied all hunger, attains to liberation even in this life. . . .

The Self is not to be known by the weak, nor by the thoughtless, nor by those who do not rightly meditate. But by the rightly meditative, the thoughtful, and the strong, he is fully known.

Having known the Self, the sages are filled with joy. Blessed are they, tranquil of mind, free from passion. Realizing everywhere the all-pervading Brahman, deeply absorbed in contemplation of his being, they enter into him, the Self of all.

[III. ii. 1-5]

Taittiriya

Let your conduct be marked by right action, including study and teaching of the scriptures; by truthfulness in word, deed, and thought; by self-denial and the practice of austerity; by poise and self-control; by performance of the everyday duties of life with a cheerful heart and an unattached mind.

Speak the truth. Do your duty. Do not neglect the study of the scriptures. Do not cut the thread of progeny. Swerve not from truth. Deviate not from the path of good. Revere greatness.

Let your mother be a god to you; let your father be a god to you; let your teacher be a god to you; let your guest also be a god to you. Do only such actions as are blameless. Always show reverence to the great.

Whatever you give to others, give with love and reverence. Gifts must be given in abundance, with joy, humility, and compassion.

If at any time there is any doubt with regard to right conduct, follow the practice of great souls, who are guileless, of good judgment, and devoted to truth.

Thus conduct yourself always. This is the injunction, this is the teaching, and this is the command of the scriptures.

[I. xi]

Aitareya

Before creation, all that existed was the Self, the Self alone. Nothing else was. Then the Self thought: "Let me send forth the worlds."

He sent forth these worlds: *Ambhas*, the highest world, above the sky and upheld by it; *Marichi,* the sky; *Mara,* the mortal world, the earth; and *Apa,* the world beneath the earth.

He thought: "Behold the worlds. Let me now send forth their guardians." Then he sent forth their guardians.

He thought: "Behold these worlds and the guardians of these worlds. Let me send forth food for the guardians." Then he sent forth food for them.

He thought: "How shall there be guardians and I have no part in them?

"If, without me, speech utters, breath is drawn, eye sees, ear hears, skin feels, mind thinks, sex organs procreate, then what am I?"

He thought: "Let me enter the guardians." Whereupon, opening the center of their skulls, he entered. The door by which he entered is called the door of bliss.*

[I. i.; iii. 11-12]

Chandogya

Within the city of Brahman, which is the body, there is the heart, and within the heart there is a little house. This house has the shape of a lotus, and within it dwells that which is to be sought after, inquired about, and realized.

What then is that which, dwelling within this little house, this lotus of the heart, is to be sought after, inquired about, and realized?

As large as the universe outside, even so large is the universe within the lotus of the heart. Within it are heaven and earth, the sun, the moon, the lightning, and all the stars. What is in the macrocosm is in this microcosm.

All things that exist, all beings and all desires, are in the city of Brahman; what then becomes of them when old age approaches and the body dissolves in death?

Though old age comes to the body, the lotus of the heart does not grow old. At death of the body, it does not die. The lotus of the heart, where Brahman exists in all his glory—that, and not the body, is the true city of Brahman. Brahman, dwelling therein, is untouched by any deed, ageless, deathless, free from grief, free from hunger and from thirst. His desires are right desires, and his desires are fulfilled.

[VIII, i. 1-5]

It was said of old:

The Self, which is free from impurities, from old age and death, from grief, from hunger and thirst, which desires nothing but what it ought to desire, and resolves nothing but what it ought to re-

---

* The sages declare that this door of bliss, the highest center of spiritual consciousness, technically known as the *sahashrara,* the thousand-petaled lotus, is situated in subtle form in the center of the brain. When the yogi, absorbed in meditation, contacts this center, he realizes his unity with Brahman.

solve, is to be sought after, is to be inquired about, is to be realized. He who learns about the Self and realizes it obtains all the worlds and all desires.

The gods and demons both heard of this truth, and they thought to themselves, "Let us seek after and realize this Self, so that we may obtain all the worlds and all desires."

Thereupon Indra from the gods, and Virochana from the demons, went to Prajapati, the renowned teacher. For thirty-two years they lived with him as pupils. Then Prajapati asked them why they had both lived with him so long.

"We have heard," they replied, "that one who realizes the Self obtains all the worlds and all desires. We have lived here because we want to learn of this Self."

Then said Prajapati: "That which is seen in the eye—that is the Self. That is immortal, that is fearless, and that is Brahman."

"Sir," inquired the disciples, "is that the Self which is seen reflected in the water, or in a mirror?"

"The Self is indeed seen reflected in these," was the reply. Then Prajapati added, "Look at yourselves in the water, and whatever you do not understand, come and tell me about it."

Indra and Virochana gazed on their reflections in the water, and returning to the sage, they said: "Sir, we have seen the Self; we have seen even the hair and the nails."

Then Prajapati bade them don their finest clothes and look again in the water. This they did, and returning to the sage, they said: "We have seen the Self, exactly like ourselves, well adorned and in our finest clothes."

To which Prajapati rejoined: "The Self is indeed seen in these. The Self is immortal and fearless, and it is Brahman." And the pupils went away well pleased.

But Prajapati, looking after them, lamented thus: "Both of them departed without analyzing or discriminating, and without truly comprehending the Self. Whosoever follows a false doctrine of the Self will perish."

[VIII. vii. viii. 1-4]

[Virochana remained satisfied with this doctrine and returned to teach that the body alone is to be worshiped. "This doctrine," says the Upanishad, "is in very truth the doctrine of the demons!" But

Indra, realizing the uselessness and falsity of such knowledge, re-
turned to Prajapati for further instruction. After another period of
thirty-two years, his teacher taught him thus:—Ed.]

"That which moves about in dreams, enjoying sensuous delights
and clothed in glory, that is the Self. That is immortal, that is
fearless, and that is Brahman."

Pleased with what he had heard, Indra again departed. But before he had reached the other gods he realized the uselessness of
this knowledge also. "True it is," he thought to himself, "that this
Self is not blind when the body is blind, nor lame or hurt when
the body is lame or hurt. But even in dreams it is conscious of
many sufferings. So in this doctrine also I can see no good."

So he went back to Prajapati for further instruction. Prajapati
now bade him live with him for another thirty-two years, and when
the time had passed taught him, saying, "When a man is sound
asleep, free from dreams, and at perfect rest—that is the Self. The
Self is immortal and fearless, and it is Brahman."

Indra went away. But before he had reached his home, he felt
the uselessness even of this knowledge. "In reality," thought he,
"one does not know oneself as this or as that while asleep. One
is not conscious, in fact, of any existence at all. The state of one in
deep sleep is next to annihilation. I can see no good in this knowledge either."

So once more Indra went back to Prajapati, who bade him stay
with him yet five years, and when the time had passed, made
known to him the highest truth of the Self, saying: "This body is
mortal, always gripped by death, but within it dwells the immortal
Self. This Self, when associated in our consciousness with the body,
is subject to pleasure and pain; and so long as this association continues, freedom from pleasure and pain can no man find. But as
this association ceases, there cease also the pleasure and the pain.

"Rising above physical consciousness, knowing the Self to be
distinct from the senses and the mind—knowing it in its true light
—one rejoices and is free."

The gods, the luminous ones, meditate on the Self, and by so
doing obtain all the worlds and all desires. In like manner, whosoever among mortals knows the Self, meditates upon it, and realizes
it—he too obtains all the worlds and all desires.

[VIII. x.-xii]

Brihadaranyaka

PEACE CHANT

OM . . .
Filled with Brahman are the things we see,
Filled with Brahman are the things we see not,
From out of Brahman floweth all that is:
From Brahman all—yet is he still the same.
OM . . . Peace—peace—peace.

Lead me from the unreal to the real.
Lead me from darkness to light.
Lead me from death to immortality.

[V. i. 1; I. iii. 28]

Yagnavalkya (to his wife)

Maitreyi, I am resolved to renounce the world and begin the life of renunciation. I wish therefore to divide my property between you and my other wife, Katyayani.

Maitreyi

My lord, if this whole earth belonged to me, with all its wealth, should I through its possession attain immortality?

Yagnavalkya

No. Your life would be like that of the rich. None can possibly hope to attain immortality through wealth.

Maitreyi

Then what need have I of wealth? Please, my lord, tell me what you know about the way to immortality.

Yagnavalkya

Dear to me have you always been, Maitreyi, and now you ask to learn of that truth which is nearest my heart. Come, sit by me. I will explain it to you. Meditate on what I say.

It is not for the sake of the husband, my beloved, that the husband is dear, but for the sake of the Self.

It is not for the sake of the wife, my beloved, that the wife is dear, but for the sake of the Self.

It is not for the sake of the children, my beloved, that the children are dear, but for the sake of the Self. . . .

The Self, beloved Maitreyi, is to be known. Hear about it, reflect upon it, meditate upon it. By knowing the Self, my beloved, through hearing, reflection, and meditation, one comes to know all things. . . .

As a lump of salt when thrown into water melts away and the lump cannot be taken out, but wherever we taste the water it is salty, even so, O Maitreyi, the individual self, dissolved, is the Eternal—pure consciousness, infinite and transcendent. Individuality arises by identification of the Self, through ignorance, with the elements; and with the disappearance of consciousness of the many, in divine illumination, it disappears. Where there is consciousness of the Self, individuality is no more.

This it is, O my beloved, that I wanted to tell you.

Maitreyi

"Where there is consciousness of the Self, individuality is no more": this that you say, my lord, confuses me.

Yagnavalkya

My beloved, let nothing I have said confuse you. But meditate well the truth that I have spoken.

As long as there is duality, one sees *the other,* one hears *the other,* one smells *the other,* one speaks to *the other,* one thinks of *the other,* one knows *the other;* but when for the illumined soul the all is dissolved in the Self, who is there to be seen by whom, who is there to be smelt by whom, who is there to be heard by whom, who is there to be spoken to by whom, who is there to be thought of by whom, who is there to be known by whom? Ah, Maitreyi, my beloved, the Intelligence which reveals all—by what shall it be revealed? By whom shall the Knower be known? The Self is described as *not this, not that.* It is incomprehensible, for it cannot be comprehended; undecaying, for it never decays; unattached, for it never attaches itself; unbound, for it is never bound. By whom, O my beloved, shall the Knower be known?

This it is that I teach you, O Maitreyi. This is the truth of immortality.

So saying, Yagnavalkya entered upon the path of renunciation.

[II. iv. 1-5, 12-14]

*   *   *

Yagnavalkya

The Self, the great unborn, the undecaying, the undying, the immortal, the fearless, is, in very truth, Brahman. He who knows Brahman is without fear. He who knows Brahman becomes Brahman!

Gods, men, and asuras—all three descendants of Prajapati—lived with him for a time as students.

Then the gods said: "Teach us, sir!" In reply Prajapati uttered one syllable: "Da." Then he said: "Have you understood?" They answered: "Yes, we have understood. You said to us, 'Damayata—Be self-controlled.'" "Yes," agreed Prajapati, "you have understood."

Then the men said: "Teach us, sir." Prajapati uttered the same syllable: "Da." Then he said: "Have you understood?" They answered, "Yes, we have understood. You said to us, 'Datta—Be charitable.'" "Yes," agreed Prajapati, "you have understood."

Then the asuras said: "Teach us, sir." Prajapati uttered the same syllable: "Da." Then he said: "Have you understood?" They said, "Yes, we have understood. You told us 'Dayadhwam—Be compassionate.'" "Yes," agreed Prajapati, "you have understood."

The storm cloud thunders: "Da! Da! Da!—Be self-controlled! Be charitable! Be compassionate!"

[IV. iv. 25; V. ii]

Svetasvatara

This vast universe is a wheel. Upon it are all creatures that are subject to birth, death, and rebirth. Round and round it turns, and never stops. It is the wheel of Brahman. As long as the individual self thinks it is separate from Brahman, it revolves upon the wheel in bondage to the laws of birth, death, and rebirth. But when through the grace of Brahman it realizes its identity with him, it revolves upon the wheel no longer. It achieves immortality.

[I. 6]

Matter is perishable. The Lord, the destroyer of ignorance, is imperishable, immortal. He is the one God, the Lord of the perishable and of all souls. By meditating on him, by uniting oneself with him, by identifying oneself with him, one ceases to be ignorant.

Know God, and all fetters will be loosed. Ignorance will vanish. Birth, death, and rebirth will be no more. Meditate upon him and transcend physical consciousness. Thus will you reach union with the lord of the universe. Thus will you become identified with him who is One without a second. In him all your desires will find fulfillment.

The truth is that you are always united with the Lord. But you must *know* this. Nothing further is there to know. Meditate, and you will realize that mind, matter, and Maya [the power which unites mind and matter] are but three aspects of Brahman, the one reality.

Fire, though present in the firesticks, is not perceived until one stick is rubbed against another. The Self is like that fire: it is realized in the body by meditation on the sacred syllable OM.

Let your body be the stick that is rubbed, the sacred syllable OM the stick that is rubbed against it. Thus shall you realize God, who is hidden within the body as fire is hidden within the wood.

Like oil in sesame seeds, butter in cream, water in the river bed, fire in tinder, the Self dwells within the soul. Realize him through truthfulness and meditation.

Like butter in cream is the Self in everything. Knowledge of the Self is gained through meditation. The Self is Brahman. By Brahman is all ignorance destroyed.

[I. 10-16]

*   *   *

Thou art woman, thou art man,
Thou art the youth, thou art the maiden,

Thou art the old man tottering with his staff;
Thou facest everywhere.

Thou art the dark butterfly,
Thou art the green parrot with red eyes,
Thou art the thunder cloud, the seasons, the seas.
Without beginning art thou,
Beyond time, beyond space.
Thou art he from whom sprang
The three worlds.

Maya is thy divine consort—
Wedded to thee.
Thou art her master, her ruler.
Red, white, and black is she,
Each color a guna.
Many are her children—
The rivers, the mountains,
Flower, stone, and tree,
Beast, bird, and man—
In every way like herself.
Thou, spirit in flesh,
Forgetting what thou art,
Unitest with Maya—
But only for a season.
Parting from her at last,
Thou regainest thyself.[1]

[IV. 3-5]

NOTE

1. From Swami Prabhavananda and Frederick Manchester, translators, *The Upanishads: Breath of the Eternal* (1947).

I I

THE EPICS

4. The Ramayana

The *Ramayana* is considered to be the first poetical work of purely human origin in the literature of India. Its traditional author is Valmiki, a highway robber who, through the mediation of the divine sage Narada, was transformed into an epic poet and saint.

The story of the *Ramayana,* like many other Indian religious works, is deeply complex, ethical, and at times surpassingly beautiful. The early part of the poem concerns the upbringing of Rama and his stepbrothers Bharata, Lakshmana, and Shatrughna; and Rama's exile to the forest with his wife Sita and Lakshmana. The circumstances leading to this event are as follows: shortly after Rama's marriage to Sita, the king decided to give up his throne and make Rama the prince regent. The people rejoiced at his decision. But a wicked maid encouraged Rama's stepmother, Queen Kaikeyi, to take advantage of two boons which the king had previously offered her. Thereupon the queen insisted that the boons be granted. To satisfy the first one, she asked that Rama be banished for fourteen years; for the other, that her son Bharata gain the throne in Rama's place. The king, a devotee of truth and loyal to his word (one of the prime lessons of the *Ramayana*) reluctantly agreed to her demand. He later died from grief.

The latter part of the story concerns the capture of Sita by Ravana, the demon king of Ceylon, and the long struggle to free her with the help of Hanuman, one of Rama's closest disciples.

The following selection tells of the attempt of Bharata to persuade Rama to return to the capital of Ayodhya and be crowned king in his place. Of particular importance is Rama's speech to his stepbrother in which he clearly expresses the Vedantic ideal of seeking the supreme Reality in the midst of the fleeting objects of the world; at the same time, without violating the laws of the society into which one is born.

The Ramayana

The princes [Bharata and Shatrughna] surrounded by relatives and friends passed the night sorrowing. The day having dawned, the brothers observed the fire sacrifice and performed the repetition of silent prayer on the banks of the river Mandakini, then entering the hermitage of Rama, they sat in profound silence, no one uttering a word, a great peace prevailing over all.

At length, Shri Bharata, in the midst of his friends, broke the silence and thus addressed Shri Rama: "O My Brother, our illustrious sovereign conferred the kingdom on me to satisfy my mother and fulfil the obligation of his former boons, and my mother having given this kingdom to me, I now offer it to thee, enjoy it without hindrance. When the dam bursts in the rainy season, none can stem the tide, similarly none but thee can protect this vast dominion. O King, as an ass cannot equal the pace of a horse, nor an ordinary bird's flight that of an eagle, so am I unable to rule the kingdom without thee.

"O Rama, happy is the sovereign on whom others depend, but wretched is the one who depends on others. A tree planted and watered, though it grow and spread forth great branches that no dwarf can scale, and be covered with blossom, if it bear no fruit, the one who planted it suffers obloquy. O Mighty Hero, let this metaphor be understood by thee, that thou, being the Lord of all, mayst guide thy servants. O Lord, let us behold thee, the destroyer of thy foes, seated on the royal throne, shining resplendent like the sun. May these mighty tuskers follow thy chariot and all the queens dwelling in the palace rejoice."

The people hearing Shri Bharata's words applauded them saying, "Well said! Well said!"

Then the compassionate Rama perceiving Bharata afflicted and lamenting, consoled him saying: "O Bharata, man is not free, time [karma] drags him hither and thither. All objects perish, all individualised souls must depart when their merit is exhausted; sons, friends, wives, all who live must die one day. Hoarding and spending, prosperity and destitution, meeting and parting, life and death are all akin. When the ripe fruit falls, we are not surprised, thus a man being born should not fear when death claims him.

"As a building supported by stout pillars on becoming old, falls into ruins, so man subject to age, must one day meet with dissolution. O Bharata, the night once past, does not come again; so the waters of the Yamuna, flowing to the sea, do not return. See! The days and nights are passing away, decreasing the period of our life's span, as the rays of the sun in summer suck up the earth's moisture. O Prince, grieve for thyself therefore, there is nought else worthy of grief! Age withers all whether movable or immovable. Death is ever at our side, nor does it leave us when we travel to a distant place, and it is still present at our returning!

"What shall a man do when his skin is wrinkled and grey hair covers his head and he is stricken in years? Man rejoices when the sun rises and sets, heedless of the waning of his powers. He welcomes the approach of each season, such as the arrival of spring, yet the succession of the seasons devours man's days! As pieces of driftwood, floating on the sea, come together for a space, so wives, sons, relatives, wealth and property remain with us a while, but in the course of time, leave us.

"One, sitting by the wayside, cries to a group of travellers passing by, 'Let me also go with you!' Why then should man grieve to tread the road which has been trodden by his predecessors? The life of man, like a river flowing, does not return, thus our days diminish and we should perform those righteous acts that bring us to the knowledge of Reality.

"Practising virtue, man should enjoy worldly pleasures; our father, the illustrious Dasharatha, having performed benevolent deeds and given fitting charitable gifts, has departed, clothed in virtue. Having cherished his servants and nourished his people, having levied those taxes alone warranted by moral duty, having set up water tanks and created reservoirs and performed many sacrificial acts, he has passed away. Leaving the world after enjoying a variety of pleasures and offering countless sacrifices, the king, at a great age, has gone to heaven.

"O Brother, it is not meet to grieve for the king, who, full of years, having enjoyed the pleasures of the world, respected by the good, has given up his life. Having abandoned his worn-out frame, he has obtained the form of a celestial being.

"A wise, learned, and enlightened man like thee should not grieve for such a sire. Exercising patience, thou shouldst cease to lament, and giving up sorrow return to the capital. O Chief among the Eloquent, thy father has commanded thee to dwell in Ayodhya. I too will perform the behests of him who ever practised righteousness!

"I cannot disregard the commands of my illustrious father, he is worthy to be obeyed by thee and me, being our parent and our ruler. O Son of Raghu, I shall, therefore, obey his will and dwell in the forest. O Chief of Men, those who desire felicity in a future state, and who are virtuous and benevolent should obey their elders. O Great One, bear in mind the behests of our father, a lover of truth, and return to the capital to rule over the kingdom!"

The magnanimous Rama, having uttered these sage words relative to the need for obedience to his father, became silent.

Rama, the lover of his people, having spoken, ceased; then the pious Bharata answered Rama, putting forth persuasive arguments of righteous purport, saying: "O Lord, who is there in this world like thee? Adversity does not move thee, nor does any agreeable thing touch thee. All look on thee as their superior, yet thou seekest counsel of thine elders!

"The man to whom the living and dead are one and who is indifferent as to what he possesses or loses, for what reason should he grieve? O Lord, those who like thee, know, as thou dost, what is the nature of the soul and its essence, are not moved in the hour of distress!

"O Prince of Raghu, like the gods, thou art magnanimous, thou art ever forbearing and faithful to thy vows. Thou art wise, thou knowest and seest all! Thou art aware of the motives of men's actions and the cause of their abandoning them; therefore, that distress which is insupportable to others, does not, in any wise, disturb thee."

Having spoken thus, Bharata continued: "O Rama, be gracious to me, though during my absence in a strange land, my mother committed those sins which cause my affliction. I am bound by the ties of duty, else I would have slain my wicked mother. What is evil and what is good is known to me, descended as I am from the righteous King Dasharatha, therefore I am unable to act contrary to virtue. I cannot speak evil in the assembly of my pious and aged father, who has passed away, and where is a man to be found so wholly acquainted with the law of righteousness as was the king, yet what person familiar with the moral law, would commit so great a wrong prompted by the desire to please a woman? There is an ancient saying that, at the approach of death, man loses the power of judgment! The king has verily justified this adage to the whole world! Through fear of Queen Kaikeyi's wrath or her threat of self-imposed destruction, or through mental agitation, the king may have acted thus without consulting his subjects, but thou art not bound by such a deed. He who imputes the transgressions of his father to righteous motives is not considered a good son; as heir to the king, reveal not the errors of thy sire, but conceal this unjust deed from the world.

"O Hero, it is thy duty to save my mother Kaikeyi, my father, my relatives and myself from the consequences of this action condemned by all. O Brother, remember thy duty as a warrior and reflect on the outcome of thy sojourn in the forest as an ascetic, but do thou also consider the good of thy people. It becomes thee not to undertake this course of action. The first duty of a warrior is to be installed so that he may be able to protect his people. Say, why should a man giving up that which is an established duty, embrace that which is wretched, cheerless, visionary and undefined? If, O Blessed One, thou desirest to undertake this mortification, why dost thou not seek it through the arduous labour of ruling the four castes? It is said that the duty of the householder is the highest dharma. Then why dost thou abandon it?

"O Lord, hear me; I am but thy child in respect of learning, age and state. How should I be able to govern the kingdom? I, a child, void of understanding and virtue and in rank also thine inferior; how should I be able to live without thee much less rule in thy stead? Therefore, O Raghava, O Thou Virtuous One, do thou, with thy relatives govern the kingdom without opposition and acquire merit! The great sage, the Holy Vasishtha, is here present with the ministers and priests. Permit thyself to be crowned and return with us to Ayodhya!

"As Indra, having conquered his foes, entered heaven attended by the Maruts, do thou enter Ayodhya, thereby discharging thy duties to the gods, the sages, and thine ancestors, gratifying the ambitions of thy friends! Regard me as thy servant and command me! O Noble One, let thy friends to-day rejoice at thine enthronement and let the evil doers flee to the uttermost ends of the earth! O Chief of Men, wash away the taint of my mother's guilt and deliver our great parent from this heinous sin. With my head bent in submission, I entreat thee; as Shri Vishnu shows his compassion to all beings, do thou show mercy to us. Shouldst thou however reject my prayer and go hence to some other forest, then will I follow thee there!"

Shri Rama, thus entreated by Shri Bharata, who had placed his head at the feet of his brother in humility, still remained steadfast in his vow and did not waver or consent to return to Ayodhya. Beholding the constancy of Shri Rama, all present rejoiced to see him so faithful to his vow, yet bewailed his determination not to return to the capital.[1]

[*Ayodhya Kanda,* 105-106]

NOTE

1. From Hari Prasad Shastri, translator, *The Ramayana of Valmiki,* Vol. I (1957).

5. The Mahabharata

The *Mahabharata,* whose reputed author is the sage Vyasa, was most likely the work of many authors. In its final form it runs to some two hundred thousand verses, making it the longest epic in the world. Comprising a rich collection of stories, legends, and teachings, the *Mahabharata* reflects two thousand years of India's cultural and religious heritage. It is unparalleled as a treasure house of Indian spiritual and secular lore.

The story of the *Mahabharata* takes place in the ancient kingdom of the Kurus, an area near modern Delhi. Its central theme concerns the struggle between two royal families—the Kauravas and Pandavas—for control of the kingdom. After the death of King Pandu, his five sons are placed under the protective custody of his brother, Dhritarashtra. Almost immediately Duryodhana, eldest of Dhritarashtra's hundred sons, is filled with an intense jealousy toward the noble and pious Pandavas. Next follows a series of adventures and plottings in which Duryodhana attempts to destroy the Pandavas and thereby secure the kingdom for himself. The conflict finally culminates in a great battle at Kurukshetra, which forms the background for the *Bhagavad-Gita* and its famous dialogue between Arjuna, one of the Pandavas, and Sri Krishna.

In the *Shanti Parva* (Book of Peace), which takes up most of the present section, the scene is the aftermath of the Pandava victory at Kurukshetra. Bhishma, the noble grandsire of the Pandavas and a great warrior, lies dying. His advice to Yudhisthira, the eldest Pandava, is a summary of the virtues expected not only of India's ancient kings, but of the spiritual aspirant as well.

The Mahabharata

Shanti Parva

King Yudhisthira, brooding over the loss of his sons, grandsons, and kinsmen killed in battle, was weighed down with grief. The thought of again ruling a kingdom disgusted him. But at last, persuaded by Sri Krishna, the noble Vyasa, and others, he returned to the city of Hastinapura [to be crowned]. And there, seated with his wife Draupadi, he was annointed by Krishna as king.

Then Yudhisthira sent the assembly away. Smiling, he approached Sri Krishna.

Yudhisthira
O Lord, whose valor pervades the three worlds, by your grace we have received back our kingdom, and the world is under our control.

But Krishna was deeply absorbed in contemplation, and gave the king no reply.

Yudhisthira
Wonder of wonders! You, the mighty one, what is it that you are thinking about?

Krishna
I am thinking of Bhishma, lying on a bed of arrows, who is now dying like the fading embers of a fire, and who is absorbed in thought of me; my mind, therefore, is also in him. He is the greatest of those who know the *dharmas*. When he is dead, Yudhisthira, the world will be swallowed in darkness like the night which has lost the moon. Therefore, approach him with reverence and inquire of him what you desire to know. Such knowledge will die with him—hence, I urge you to see him.

Therefore Yudhisthira, Krishna, and the other Pandavas mounted their horses and sped to the field at Kurukshetra, where they found Bhishma lying by the bank of the Oghavati on a bed of arrows.

Krishna

O ruler of men, through your wisdom remove that sorrow which has infected Yudhisthira. For men such as you, possessed of true wisdom, banish man's bewilderment and strife.

Bhishma

Meditating on thee, O Krishna, the energy of youth has returned to me. By thy grace I am able to speak out what would bring good to all.

O Yudhisthira, exert yourself always. Human endeavor is greater than dependence on fate [karma]. He who depends on fate only grows confused.

Be straightforward in all actions; truthfulness always brings success.

From all quarters people take advantage of a king who is soft-hearted; if too harsh, people become fearful of him. Therefore, balance these qualities in your life. Be addicted to nothing.

The duty of a king is to engage himself in doing good to the world, sacrificing his own pleasures.

The best king is he whose countrymen live under him without fear, like sons in the house of their father.

The king must conquer his own self completely. Only then will his enemies be conquered.

He should avoid lust and anger. He must follow the path of duty and bring economic security to all.

If, against the injunctions of the scriptures, the king heavily taxes his subject—motivated by the hope of gaining wealth for himself—he brings about his own ruin.

My son, never oppress the poor and downtrodden; remember the tears that fall from the falsely accused soon destroy the sons and cattle of the oppressor.

A king should seek to retain his power by any means other than war. Victory bought at the expense of battle is the basest of all victories.

Treat others as thou wouldst thyself be treated.

Greed is the root cause of sin. Therefore, the self-controlled person constantly seeks to destroy avarice and the delusion it fosters.

He who is always a friend of others and by his word, thought, and deed is continually engrossed in doing good to others knows the meaning of dharma.

Passion, hatred, melancholy, anger, pride, delusion, laziness, and envy—these constitute ignorance. Forbearance, bravery, non-injury, truthfulness, calmness, affection, steadiness of mind, and freedom from envy—these constitute self-control. There is no higher virtue than self-control.

Truthfulness is the eternal dharma. Truth is the eternal *Brahman*. Truthfulness is the greatest offering one can make to God. Truthfulness is the support of all things.

These are the various kinds of truthfulness: truthfulness of speech, calmness, absence of jealousy, forbearance, modesty, endurance, freedom from spite, renunciation, meditation, freedom from the effects of happiness and misery, compassion, and non-injury.

That happiness which is derived from fulfillment of worldly desires and that greater happiness which one may obtain in heaven are not equal to even one-sixteenth of the happiness gained through the stilling of desire.

When a man draws in his senses as the tortoise draws in its legs—then the light and splendor of the soul begin to shine within.

When man goes beyond liking and disliking, when fear has left him and he makes others fearless—then does a man become Brahman. When a man does not injure any being in thought, word, or deed—then does a man become Brahman.

Death stalks this world, and old age envelops it. Days and nights march relentlessly on. Why do you not awake? Even now do what would bring you good; let not time pass you. Now, with so much still left undone, death beckons you.

Death and eternal life—both abide in the body. Death comes through delusion; immortality, by the path of truth.

There is no sight equal to learning, no austerity equal to truthfulness, no misery like passion, and no happiness equal to following the ideal of renunciation.

Constant association with riches creates delusion and pride.

Without renunciation, happiness is not possible; without renunciation, one cannot even rest without fear; without renunciation, one does not attain the Supreme Truth. By giving up everything, one knows true happiness.

The happy man is he who is always tranquil, free of worry, truthful in speech, scornful of worldly things, and beyond any desire.

Even when a thing much-prized is attained, we are not content; the fire of greed cannot be quenched by fulfillment of any object of desire, but blazes forth all the more.

The secret meaning of the Vedas is truth; of truth, self-control; of self-control, freedom from all bondage. This is the sum of all scriptures.[1]

From *Vana Parva*

Alms-giving is the way to fame, truthfulness is the way to heaven, right conduct is the way to happiness. The best of gains is the gaining of health, and the best of happiness is contentment.   [313.70]

There is no greater virtue than kindness. They who have their minds under control never come to grief. Friendship with the holy never ages.   [313.76]

He who gives up vanity is loved by all. He who gives up anger never grieves. He who gives up greed becomes happy.   [313.78]

Kindness is desiring happiness for all. Straightforwardness is mental poise. Holy is he who is kind to all. Wicked is he who is cruel.   [313.90]

From *Anushasana Parva*

Do nothing to thy neighbour which hereafter thou wouldst not have thy neighbour do to thee.   [113.8]

Man should always worship God with devotion—this I consider the greatest of all truths.   [149.8]

The blessed ones who love the Lord and are devoted to him are free from anger, malice, avarice, and evil thought.   [149.33]

Purity of conduct is the greatest purity. To think of God continuously, to worship him, to chant his name and sing his praises—this is the best way of attaining the highest good.[2]   [108.12]

NOTES

1. Translated by Swami Prabhavananda and Clive Johnson.
2. Translated by Swami Prabhavananda and Frederick Manchester in Swami Prabhavananda, *The Spiritual Heritage of India* (1964).

6. Bhagavad-Gita

By far the best known part of the *Mahabharata* is the *Bhagavad-Gita* or "Song of God," whose seven hundred verses vividly dramatize the quest of man for deliverance from suffering and a way to eternal peace and freedom. One can say, without fear of contradiction, that the Gita has come to be regarded among all classes of India's people as the Bible of Hinduism. And yet its message is not confined simply to the Hindu. The Gita is a scripture of universal scope, the spirit of whose teachings is found in nearly every religion of the world.

Indian thought has been too often identified with the impersonal ideal of nondualism. But Hinduism is equally concerned with the ideal of devotion to a personal God. One of the greatnesses of the Gita is its ability to synthesize the four yogas or paths to God into a cohesive whole. Thus the perfect man, according to the Gita, is a blending of intellectual discrimination (*jnana yoga*), devotion to God (*bhakti yoga*), selfless action (*karma yoga*), and one-pointed meditation (*raja yoga*). He is harmonious and well-balanced.

Most scholars date the Gita somewhere between the second and fifth centuries before Christ. Although, according to some, its significance places it in the category of *Shruti,* or revealed scriptures, it is regarded as *Smriti* (literally, to "fix in the memory") and as an expression of the essential teachings of the Upanishads.

The historical setting of the Gita is a battlefield on the plain of Kurukshetra. It begins on the eve of the decisive confrontation between the Kauravas and the Pandavas. Before the battle, Arjuna, the great epic hero and leader of the Pandavas, suddenly refuses to fight, explaining to his mentor and charioteer, Sri Krishna, that he cannot reconcile his duty as a warrior with the act of killing kinsmen and friends. The remainder of the Gita's eighteen chapters consists of Sri Krishna's answers to the questions of his disciple concerning the meaning of life. The result is an inspiring book of instruction on the way of attaining knowledge of God—the Self—and release from the bondage of ignorance.

Bhagavad-Gita

The Yoga of Knowledge

Arjuna

Bhishma and Drona* are noble and ancient, worthy of the deepest reverence. How can I greet them with arrows, in battle? If I kill them, how can I ever enjoy my wealth, or any other pleasure? It will be cursed with blood-guilt. I would much rather spare them, and eat the bread of a beggar.

Which will be worse, to win this war, or to lose it? I scarcely know. Even the sons of Dhritarashtra stand in the enemy ranks. If we kill them, none of us will wish to live.

Is this real compassion that I feel, or only a delusion? My mind gropes about in darkness. I cannot see where my duty lies. Krishna, I beg you, tell me frankly and clearly what I ought to do. I am your disciple. I put myself into your hands. Show me the way.

> Not this world's kingdom,
> Supreme, unchallenged,
> No, nor the throne
> Of the gods in heaven,
> Could ease this sorrow
> That numbs my senses!

*   *   *

Sri Krishna

Your words are wise, Arjuna, but your sorrow is for nothing. The truly wise mourn neither for the living nor for the dead.

There was never a time when I did not exist, nor you, nor any of these kings. Nor is there any future in which we shall cease to be.

Just as the dweller in this body passes through childhood, youth

---

* Commanders of the opposing army.

and old age, so at death he merely passes into another kind of body. The wise are not deceived by that.

Feelings of heat and cold, pleasure and pain, are caused by the contact of the senses with their objects. They come and they go, never lasting long. You must accept them.

A serene spirit accepts pleasure and pain with an even mind, and is unmoved by either. He alone is worthy of immortality. . . .

That Reality which pervades the universe is indestructible. No one has power to change the Changeless.

Bodies are said to die, but That which possesses the body is eternal. It cannot be limited, or destroyed. Therefore you must fight.

> Some say this Atman
> Is slain, and others
> Call It the slayer:
> They know nothing.
> How can It slay
> Or who shall slay It?

> Know this Atman
> Unborn, undying,
> Never ceasing,
> Never beginning,
> Deathless, birthless,
> Unchanging for ever.
> How can It die
> The death of the body?

> Knowing It birthless,
> Knowing It deathless,
> Knowing It endless,
> For ever unchanging,
> Dream not you do
> The deed of the killer,
> Dream not the power
> Is yours to command it.

> Worn-out garments
> Are shed by the body:

Worn-out bodies
Are shed by the dweller
Within the body.
New bodies are donned
By the dweller, like garments.

Not wounded by weapons,
Not burned by fire,
Not dried by the wind,
Not wetted by water:
Such is the Atman,

Not dried, not wetted,
Not burned, not wounded,
Innermost element,
Everywhere, always,
Being of beings,
Changeless, eternal,
For ever and ever.

*   *   *

Arjuna

Krishna, how can one identify a man who is firmly established and absorbed in Brahman? In what manner does an illumined soul speak? How does he sit? How does he walk?

Sri Krishna

He knows bliss in the Atman
And wants nothing else.
Cravings torment the heart:
He renounces cravings.
I call him illumined.

Not shaken by adversity,
Not hankering after happiness:
Free from fear, free from anger,
Free from the things of desire.
I call him a seer, and illumined.

The bonds of his flesh are broken.
He is lucky, and does not rejoice:
He is unlucky, and does not weep.
I call him illumined.

The tortoise can draw in his legs:
The seer can draw in his senses.
I call him illumined.

The abstinent run away from what they desire
But carry their desires with them:
When a man enters Reality,
He leaves his desires behind him.

Even a mind that knows the path
Can be dragged from the path:
The senses are so unruly.
But he controls the senses
And recollects the mind
And fixes it on me.
I call him illumined.

Thinking about sense-objects
Will attach you to sense-objects;
Grow attached, and you become addicted;
Thwart your addiction, it turns to anger;
Be angry, and you confuse your mind;
Confuse your mind, you forget the lesson of experience;
Forget experience, you lose discrimination;
Lose discrimination, and you miss life's only purpose.

When he has no lust, no hatred,
A man walks safely among the things of lust and hatred.
To obey the Atman
Is his peaceful joy:
Sorrow melts
Into that clear peace:
His quiet mind
Is soon established in peace.

The uncontrolled mind
Does not guess that the Atman is present:
How can it meditate?
Without meditation, where is peace?
Without peace, where is happiness?

The wind turns a ship
From its course upon the waters:
The wandering winds of the senses
Cast man's mind adrift
And turn his better judgment from its course.
When a man can still the senses
I call him illumined.

The recollected mind is awake
In the knowledge of the Atman
Which is dark night to the ignorant:
The ignorant are awake in their sense-life
Which they think is daylight:
To the seer it is darkness.

Water flows continually into the ocean
But the ocean is never disturbed:
Desire flows into the mind of the seer
But he is never disturbed.
The seer knows peace:

The man who stirs up his own lusts
Can never know peace.
He knows peace who has forgotten desire.
He lives without craving:
Free from ego, free from pride.

This is the state of enlightenment in Brahman:
A man does not fall back from it
Into delusion.
Even at the moment of death
He is alive in that enlightenment:
Brahman and he are one.

[II. 4-8; 11-15; 17-24; 54-72]

Renunciation Through Knowledge

Sri Krishna

What is action? What is inaction? Even the wise are puzzled by this question. Therefore, I will tell you what action is. When you know that, you will be free from all impurity. You must learn what kind of work to do, what kind of work to avoid, and how to reach a state of calm detachment from your work. The real nature of action is hard to understand.

He who sees the inaction that is in action, and the action that is in inaction, is wise indeed. Even when he is engaged in action he remains poised in the tranquillity of the Atman.

The seers say truly
That he is wise
Who acts without lust or scheming
For the fruit of the act:
His act falls from him,
Its chain is broken,
Melted in the flame of my knowledge.
Turning his face from the fruit,
He needs nothing:
The Atman is enough.
He acts, and is beyond action.

Not hoping, not lusting,
Bridling body and mind,
He calls nothing his own:
He acts, and earns no evil.

What God's Will gives
He takes, and is contented.
Pain follows pleasure,
He is not troubled:
Gain follows loss,
He is indifferent:
Of whom should he be jealous?
He acts, and is not bound by his action.

When the bonds are broken
His illumined heart
Beats in Brahman:
His every action
Is worship of Brahman:
Can such acts bring evil?

Brahman is the ritual,
Brahman is the offering,
Brahman is he who offers
To the fire that is Brahman.
If a man sees Brahman
In every action,
He will find Brahman.*

[IV. 16-24]

The Yoga of Meditation

Sri Krishna

When can a man be said to have achieved union with Brahman?
When his mind is under perfect control and freed from all desires,
so that he becomes absorbed in the Atman, and nothing else.
"The light of a lamp does not flicker in a windless place": that
is the simile which describes a yogi of one-pointed mind, who
meditates upon the Atman. When, through the practise of yoga,
the mind ceases its restless movements, and becomes still, he realizes
the Atman. It satisfies him entirely. Then he knows that infinite
happiness which can be realized by the purified heart but is beyond
the grasp of the senses. He stands firm in this realization. Because
of it, he can never again wander from the inmost truth of his
being.

Now that he holds it
He knows this treasure
Above all others:
Faith so certain

* This verse is chanted by all Hindu monks as a grace before meals. In
this instance, "the fire" is regarded as the fire of hunger.

Shall never be shaken
By heaviest sorrow.

To achieve this certainty is to know the real meaning of the word yoga. It is the breaking of contact with pain. You must practise this yoga resolutely, without losing heart. Renounce all your desires, for ever. They spring from wilfulness. Use your discrimination to restrain the whole pack of the scattering senses.

Patiently, little by little, a man must free himself from all mental distractions, with the aid of the intelligent will. He must fix his mind upon the Atman, and never think of anything else. No matter where the restless and the unquiet mind wanders, it must be drawn back and made to submit to the Atman only.

Utterly quiet,
Made clean of passion,
The mind of the yogi
Knows that Brahman,
His bliss is the highest.

Released from evil
His mind is constant
In contemplation:
The way is easy,
Brahman has touched him,
That bliss is boundless.

His heart is with Brahman,
His eye in all things
Sees only Brahman
Equally present,
Knows his own Atman
In every creature,
And all creation
Within that Atman.

That yogi sees me in all things, and all things within me. He never loses sight of me, nor I of him. He is established in union with me, and worships me devoutly in all beings. That yogi abides in me, no matter what his mode of life.

Who burns with the bliss
And suffers the sorrow
Of every creature
Within his own heart,
Making his own
Each bliss and each sorrow:
Him I hold highest
Of all the yogis.

Arjuna

Krishna, you describe this yoga as a life of union with Brahman.
But I do not see how this can be permanent. The mind is so very
restless.

Restless man's mind is,
So strongly shaken
In the grip of the senses:
Gross and grown hard
With stubborn desire
For what is worldly.
How shall he tame it?
Truly, I think
The wind is no wilder.

Sri Krishna

Yes, Arjuna, the mind is restless, no doubt, and hard to subdue.
But it can be brought under control by constant practice, and by
the exercise of dispassion. Certainly, if a man has no control over
his ego, he will find this yoga difficult to master. But a self-controlled man can master it, if he struggles hard, and uses the right
means.

[VI. 18-36]

The Way to Eternal Brahman

Arjuna

Tell me, Krishna, what Brahman is. What is the Atman, and what
is the creative energy of Brahman? Explain the nature of this
relative world, and of the individual man.

Who is God who presides over action in this body, and how does He dwell here? How are you revealed at the hour of death to those whose consciousness is united with you?

Sri Krishna

Brahman is that which is immutable, and independent of any cause but Itself. When we consider Brahman as lodged within the individual being, we call Him the Atman. The creative energy of Brahman is that which causes all existences to come into being.

The nature of the relative world is mutability. The nature of the individual man is his consciousness of ego. I alone am God who presides over action, here in this body.

At the hour of death, when a man leaves his body, he must depart with his consciousness absorbed in me. Then he will be united with me. Be certain of that. Whatever a man remembers at the last, when he is leaving the body, will be realized by him in the hereafter; because that will be what his mind has most constantly dwelt on, during this life.

Therefore you must remember me at all times, and do your duty. If your mind and heart are set upon me constantly, you will come to me. Never doubt this.

Make a habit of practising meditation, and do not let your mind be distracted. In this way you will come finally to the Lord, who is the light-giver, the highest of the high.

He is all-knowing God, lord of the emperors,
Ageless, subtler far than mind's inmost subtlety,
Universal sustainer,
Shining sunlike, self-luminous.

What fashion His form has, who shall conceive of it?
He dwells beyond delusion, the dark of Maya.
On Him let man meditate
Always, for then at the last hour
Of going hence from his body he will be strong
In the strength of this yoga, faithfully followed:
The mind is firm, and the heart
So full, it hardly holds its love.

Thus he will take his leave: and now, with the life-force

Indrawn utterly, held fast between the eyebrows,
He goes forth to find his Lord,
That light-giver, who is greatest.

[VIII. 1-10]

The Yoga of Devotion

Arjuna

Some worship you with steadfast love. Others worship God the unmanifest and changeless. Which kind of devotee has the greater understanding of yoga?

Sri Krishna

Those whose minds are fixed on me in steadfast love, worshipping me with absolute faith. I consider them to have the greater understanding of yoga.

As for those others, the devotees of God the unmanifest, indefinable and changeless, they worship that which is omnipresent, constant, eternal, beyond thought's compass, never to be moved. They hold all the senses in check. They are tranquil-minded, and devoted to the welfare of humanity. They see the Atman in every creature. They also will certainly come to me.

But the devotees of the unmanifest have a harder task, because the unmanifest is very difficult for embodied souls to realize.

Quickly I come
To those who offer me
Every action,
Worship me only,
Their dearest delight,
With devotion undaunted.

Because they love me
These are my bondsmen
And I shall save them
From mortal sorrow
And all the waves
Of Life's deathly ocean.

Be absorbed in me,
Lodge your mind in me:
Thus you shall dwell in me,
Do not doubt it,
Here and hereafter.

If you cannot become absorbed in me, then try to reach me by repeated concentration. If you lack the strength to concentrate, then devote yourself to works which will please me. For, by working for my sake only, you will achieve perfection. If you cannot even do this, then surrender yourself to me altogether. Control the lusts of your heart, and renounce the fruits of every action.

Concentration which is practised with discernment is certainly better than the mechanical repetition of a ritual or a prayer. Absorption in God—to live with Him and be one with Him always—is even better than concentration. But renunciation brings instant peace to the spirit.

A man should not hate any living creature. Let him be friendly and compassionate to all. He must free himself from the delusion of "I" and "mine." He must accept pleasure and pain with equal tranquillity. He must be forgiving, ever-contented, self-controlled, united constantly with me in his meditation. His resolve must be unshakable. He must be dedicated to me in intellect and in mind. Such a devotee is dear to me.

He neither molests his fellow men, nor allows himself to become disturbed by the world. He is no longer swayed by joy and envy, anxiety and fear. Therefore he is dear to me.

[XII. 1-15]

The Yoga of Renunciation

Sri Krishna

Learn from me now,
O son of Kunti,
How man made perfect
Is one with Brahman,
The goal of wisdom.
When the mind and the heart

Are freed from delusion,
United with Brahman,
When steady will
Has subdued the senses,
When sight and taste
And sound are abandoned
Without regretting,
Without aversion;
When man seeks solitude,
Eats but little,
Curbing his speech,
His mind and his body,
Ever engaged
In his meditation
On Brahman the truth,
And full of compassion;
When he casts from him
Vanity, violence,
Pride, lust, anger
And all his possessions,
Totally free
From the sense of ego
And tranquil of heart:
That man is ready
For oneness with Brahman.
And he who dwells
United with Brahman,
Calm in mind,
Not grieving, not craving,
Regarding all men
With equal acceptance:
He loves me most dearly.

To love is to know me,
My innermost nature,
The truth that I am:
Through this knowledge he enters
At once to my Being.

All that he does
Is offered before me
In utter surrender:
My grace is upon him,
He finds the eternal,
The place unchanging.

Mentally resign all your action to me. Regard me as your dearest loved one. Know me to be your only refuge. Be united always in heart and consciousness with me.

United with me, you shall overcome all difficulties by my grace. But if your heart is full of conceit, and you do not heed me, you are lost. If, in your vanity, you say: "I will not fight," your resolve is vain. Your own nature will drive you to the act. For you yourself have created the karma that binds you. You are helpless in its power. And you will do that very thing which your ignorance seeks to avoid.

The Lord lives in the heart of every creature. He turns them round and round upon the wheel of his Maya. Take refuge utterly in him. By his grace you will find supreme peace, and the state which is beyond all change.

Now I have taught you that wisdom which is the secret of secrets. Ponder it carefully. Then act as you think best. These are the last words that I shall say to you, the deepest of all truths. I speak for your own good. You are the friend I chose and love.

Give me your whole heart,
Love and adore me,
Worship me always,
Bow to me only,
And you shall find me:
This is my promise
Who love you dearly.

Lay down all duties
In me, your refuge.
Fear no longer,
For I will save you
From sin and from bondage.

You must never tell this holy truth to anyone who lacks self-control and devotion, or who despises his teacher and mocks at me. But the man who loves me, and teaches my devotees this supreme truth of the Gita, will certainly come to me. No one can do me a higher service than this. No one on earth can be dearer to me.

And if any man meditates upon this sacred discourse of ours, I shall consider that he has worshipped me in spirit. Even if a man simply listens to these words with faith, and does not doubt them, he will be freed from his sins and reach the heaven of the righteous. . . .

Arjuna

By your grace, O Lord, my delusions have been dispelled. My mind stands firm. Its doubts are ended. I will do your bidding.[1]

[XVIII. 50-71; 73]

NOTE

1. From Swami Prabhavananda and Christopher Isherwood, translators, *The Song of God: Bhagavad-Gita* (1951).

III

AUXILIARY SCRIPTURES

7. Bhagavata Purana

With the exception of the Upanishads and the *Bhagavad-Gita,* the *Bhagavata Purana* is the most popular of Hindu scriptures. It belongs to that body of sacred writings known as *Puranas* (literally, "ancient") or scriptures written primarily to amplify and illustrate the truths of the Vedas and Upanishads by recounting various allegories, legends, and stories of India's avatars and saints. In it knowledge and devotion—the paths of jnana and bhakti—are effectively harmonized. There are eighteen Puranas, six devoted to Vishnu, six to Brahma, and six to Shiva. These three divinities, known as the Hindu Trinity, are in actuality but various manifestations of the same Spirit.

The *Bhagavata* is divided into twelve *skandhas* or books. Of these, Books Ten and Eleven are the most important. Book Ten recounts the life story of Sri Krishna, the avatar-hero of the *Bhagavad-Gita* and an incarnation of Vishnu, while Book Eleven contains Krishna's teachings to his friend Uddhava, which are some of the loftiest to be found anywhere in Hindu literature.

Bhagavata Purana

Of Religion

O revered sages, there is nothing greater or more purifying than to converse about God and his divine play. The highest religion of man is unselfish love of God. If one has this love, one attains to truly divine wisdom. Fruitless is that knowledge which is not love. Fruitless is religion itself, if it have not love. Vain indeed is all struggle for spiritual life if in one's heart there be not love.

Religion is not for the purpose of securing a place in heaven. It is an inquiry into Truth, and its ideal is the knowledge and the realization of Truth.

[I. i]

Divine Love

The God of Love exists in the hearts of all. He is our very Self, and therefore very dear to us. He is Truth. He is infinity. He is the omnipotent Lord. Hence should a man, freed from all selfish desires, his mind fixed on God, worship him alone.

Do thou, O king, meditate on him within the shrine of thine own heart, and lose thyself in the consciousness of the Divine Being.

[II. i]

Our senses, O Mother, draw us to things because we love the world. If we direct our love toward God we find divine knowledge and absolute freedom. But there are souls who find such great joy in love and in the service of the Lord that they have no concern for their own salvation. Even so, divine love ultimately brings freedom to them also.

Those who love God as dearly as themselves; those who have affection for him as for their children; those who trust him as their beloved companion, and reverence him as the teacher of all teachers; those who love him as their dear friend, and worship him as God—theirs is eternal life.

Blessed indeed are they that steadfastly devote themselves to the worship of God, for they shall attain to absolute freedom.

[III. iv]

When love is firmly established in his heart, a man becomes master of himself and a teacher of humanity. He is born anew; his ego is consumed in the fire of knowledge.

The ego is the cause of ignorance. When the ego is subdued, the spiritual consciousness shines forth in all its glory. One realizes the divine Self. The manifold universe, with all its pleasure and pain, vanishes like a dream. There remains the unitary blissful consciousness, the Atman.

Thinking of objects attracts the senses to them. The senses being attracted, the mind becomes attached. When this attachment grows in the mind, man loses all power of discrimination. Losing the power of discrimination, he becomes deluded. Being deluded, he loses all memory. All memory being lost, there is lost the knowledge of the Atman, the divine Self. The loss of this knowledge is called by the wise "losing one's own Self." What greater calamity can there be than to lose one's own Self? Everything is dear to us because of the Self. When the Self is lost, what remains?

Lustful thoughts and the desire for the things of the world— these are the greatest enemies to knowledge and to the unfold- ment of divinity. Such thoughts make man dull and ignorant. Therefore should a man shun them.

O king, know the God of Love alone; know him who is to be directly realized and who dwelleth in the hearts of all beings and things. He alone abideth forever. All else is transitory. He can be directly perceived. He is expressed in and through even the minutest cells. He is all-pervading. He is the Truth. He is pure and ever free. May I take refuge in him!

As on a dark night one sees a rope as a snake, so, because of ignorance, does one see the one absolute existence as this mani- fold universe. But as, when the light comes, the snake vanishes, so when the light of knowledge dawns, the manifold universe vanishes and there remains the Satchidananda—absolute existence, absolute knowledge, and absolute bliss.

Blessed indeed are they who meditate on the Lotus Feet of the God of Love, for they shall be free from all impurities and from bondage of the heart.

Worship him alone. Six passions there are—lust, anger, greed, pride, delusion, and jealousy—which are like ferocious sharks in the ocean of the world. Accept him as thy pilot, and cross that ocean with ease, and without fear.

[IV. iii]

A Prayer

Beyond speech and mind art thou, yet easily attainable by thy devotees;

Thou dost manifest thyself to those who worship thee in any
name or form,
If only that worship is offered thee with a sincere and devoted
heart.

*   *   *

If because of evil karma we walk the path of the unrighteous,
Deluded in the mire of ignorance,
Grant us this prayer, O Lord:
That we may sing thy name,
Which charms away all sin and evil.
The veil of ignorance, difficult indeed to lift, keeps us from seeing
thy divine face.
Thy grace and the service of great souls make possible the easy
crossing of maya.

[V. ii]

Knowledge of the Self

King Chitraketu began to practice the spiritual lessons taught
him by the divine sages Angira and Narada. Soon his mind was
illumined, and he had the vision of the God of Love. He felt
overwhelming joy in his heart, and attained peace and tranquillity.

As he continued his practices there came greater and greater
illumination, and he ultimately realized his unity with Brahman:*

"I am he, the Self of the universe, dwelling in the hearts of
all. I am the Word. I am supreme Brahman.

"I exist as the Self of the universe, and the whole universe
exists in me.

"Mind assumes three states of consciousness—waking, dreaming, and dreamless sleep. I am the witness thereof, remaining
aloof from all these states, for I am transcendental consciousness.

"The blissful Self am I, experienced by transcending the senses,
the mind, the intellect, and the ego. I am Brahman.

"As one sees oneself separate from Brahman, one comes within
the domain of maya. Thus does one become subject to birth and
death, and passes from one body to another.

* The verses that follow, spoken by the king, express his unity with God.

"It is man's greatest calamity not to comprehend the divine Self.

"Man struggles to find happiness and to end his misery in this world, but he never attains this goal so long as he remains within the limits of the states of consciousness—waking, dreaming, and dreamless sleep. By transcending these and going beyond the world of maya, he realizes the Self and attains his goal.

"He who is skillful in the practice of yoga and meditation comes to know that the supreme end of life is to realize unity with God."

[VI. iv]

Love of God

That intense love, O Lord, which the ignorant bear to worldly things, may I have the same for thee; may I have the same intensity of love for thee, but only for love's sake.

[VII. i]

Castes and Orders of Life

Sri Krishna

The Self alone is real. The world of the senses is superimposed upon it. See the one reality, the divine Self, and so liberate yourself from thinking about the world of the senses. He who knows the one reality, beyond the objective world, has true knowledge. He loves me for the sake of love and does not care even for his own salvation. Such a free soul is above all rules of conduct and beyond all orders of life. Though wise, he is childlike. Though subtle, learned, and well-versed in the Scriptures, he wanders about as one who knows nothing. He causes no fear to anyone, and he is fearful of none. If vilified, he does not return the insult but remains calm. He bears enmity towards none.

The one supreme Self dwelleth in the hearts of all beings. That one existence is seen as many beings, just as the moon appears to be many when reflected in many vessels.

The wise man regards the body as only an instrument through the help of which, by meditating on the Truth and knowing the one existence, he may become free. The delusion of many existences is removed from the man who has realized me. He sees the One in the many.

[XI. xi]

I am the Goal, I am the Way

Sri Krishna

O Uddhava, I consider him wise who sees the one Self in this manifold universe.

There is one absolute existence. On its surface appear the myriad forms of the phenomenal world like bubbles on the ocean. For a while they stay, and then they disappear. The one absolute existence, the abiding reality, remains.

The Scriptures, direct experience, authority, and inference— these are the four proofs of knowledge. Finding through all these proofs the reality of the one absolute existence, the wise man is no longer attached to transitory things. The fleeting objects of this world become to him visions and dreams.

All happiness in the objective world ends in misery. The wise do not seek happiness either here or hereafter, realizing its evanescence.

Now, O Uddhava, I shall tell thee of the philosophy of love.

Drink deep of my words, which are nectar. Study the lives and teachings of my divine incarnations, the sons of God. Learn to find joy in my worship. Sing my praises.

Being devoted to my service, worship me with thy whole soul. Ennobling also is the service to my devotees. Learn to see me in all beings.

Let all thy work be done as service unto me. With thine every word extol my divine attributes. Free thy mind from all selfish desires and offer it unto me.

Renounce all enjoyments and pleasures; make sacrifices, offer gifts, chant my name, undertake vows, and practice austerities. Do all these things for my sake alone.

Thus by surrendering thyself unto me through all thy actions, and remembering me constantly, thou shalt come to love me.

When thou hast come to love me, there will be nothing more for thee to achieve.

For when the mind is completely surrendered unto me, who am the divine Self within, the heart becomes pure and tranquil, and one attains to Truth, knowledge, dispassion, and divine power. Devoid of these is one whose mind is outgoing, seeking pleasure in objects of sense.

Truth is love. Knowledge is seeing the oneness of the Self with God. Dispassion is non-attachment to objects of sense, and divine power is the control of nature, external and internal.

The first requisites for spiritual life are these: doing no injury, truthfulness, honesty, non-attachment, modesty, abstention from wealth, faith in an after life, continence, silence, patience, forgiveness, fearlessness, physical and mental purity, chanting the name of the Lord, austerity, sacrifice, self-reliance, hospitality, surrendering of the self to me, pilgrimages, working for the good of others, and service to the teacher.

These are known in yoga as the practices of yama and niyama. These, my friend, if rightly followed, bring great spiritual unfoldment.

Calmness is a steady flow of the mind toward God.

Self-restraint is control of the organs of sense.

Patience is bearing the burden of life cheerfully.

Steadiness is overcoming the palate and the impulse of sex.

The highest charity is refraining from violence.

Austerity is the giving up of desire.

Valor is the conquest of one's own self.

To know the Truth is to see the oneness of the Self with God.

Truthfulness is true and agreeable speech as exemplified by the sages.

Purity is non-attachment to work.

Renunciation is overcoming the world.

Virtue is the treasure which men covet.

I, the supreme Lord, am the sacrifice.

The greatest gift is the gift of knowledge.

The greatest strength is the control of prana.

Fortunate is he who meditates on my divine powers.

The highest profit is in devotion to me.

Wisdom is the removal of false ideas of multiplicity and realizing the unity of the Self.

Modesty is abhorrence of evil deeds.

Excellence of character arises from disregard of worldly considerations.

Happiness is the transcending of both pleasure and pain.

Misery is hankering after pleasures of sense.

Learned is he who discriminates between bondage and freedom.

Ignorant is he who identifies himself with the body.

The right path is that which leads to me.

The wrong path is that which causes restlessness of the mind.

Heaven is the domination of sattva in the mind.

Hell is the predominance of tamas.

The teacher who has realized his oneness with me is the true friend.

He indeed is rich who is rich in virtues.

Poor is he who is discontented.

Mean is he who is not master of his senses.

Godly is he who is not attached to objects of sense.

Divine is he who has overcome both good and evil.

[XI. xii]

A Prayer

Even as rivers spring from different sources,
Yet mingle in the ocean,
So all the Vedas, all Scriptures, all Truth, though of diverse origin,
Come home to thee!¹

[VIII. i]

NOTE

1. From Swami Prabhavananda, translator, *Srimad Bhagavatam: The Wisdom of God* (1943).

8. The Tantras

Because of a general ignorance regarding their real meaning, the Tantras have been largely misunderstood in the West. Thus they have been often associated with black magic, secret mantras, and eroticism. Although these elements may be found to some extent in Tantric literature (in what is commonly known as "left-handed" Tantra), their role is so insignificant as to be of little or no importance.

According to the Tantras, the creative principle of the world is *Shakti* or God the Mother, which is united with *Shiva* or Brahman (as heat is inseparable from its power to burn). Shakti, therefore, is not indistinct from Shiva, the Absolute of the Upanishads, but is the power of the Absolute. To realize this is the purpose of Tantra.

According to Tantra, we are drawn again and again to life in the world because of our own desires—desires which require form in order to reach fulfillment. But the process is unending. For as each desire is satisfied, new ones are created. Thus is constructed a prison of our own making. We are enmeshed in a network of cravings which keeps us bound to this earth life after life.

By means of the Tantric disciplines the devotee comes to know his Brahman nature, which is *Sat-chit-ananda* [Absolute Existence, Consciousness, and Bliss]. He then becomes free from desire and lives detached from the objects of sense. Having broken the cycle of karma, he no longer returns to the world of form, but enters the ocean of immortal bliss.

The *Mahanirvana Tantra* is composed in the form of a dialogue between Shiva and his consort the goddess Parvati, and contains instructions on nearly every aspect of the religious life of ancient India. The selection in this book is a prayer to the formless

Brahman, who is seen as the sole refuge of the aspirant. The *Kularnava Tantra* is more practical in emphasis, underlining the virtues to be sought by the Tantric devotee.

The Tantras

From *Mahanirvana Tantra*

HYMN TO BRAHMAN

Within the lotus,
The heart's chamber,
There let me meditate
On Brahman, Divine Consciousness,
Who is neither this nor that
Since he is all,
Who lacks nothing
Since all powers are his.
The yogis attain him
Through meditation,
He takes away fear
Of death, rebirth,
He is Being and Knowing,
Seed of the worlds.

I bow before you,
Eternal Refuge,
I bow before you,
Awareness made visible
As this, our world;
I bow before you,
Sole Reality,
Giver of freedom;
I bow before you,
The All-Pervading
Beyond all aspects
Absolute Brahman.

For you are our only refuge,
Lord of our adoration,
Master of this universe,
Giver of light,
Maker, Sustainer, Destroyer,
Yourself changeless,
Alone, above all else.

You are the dread of the dreadful, terror of the terrible,
Refuge of all beings, purifier of all that purifies,
Supreme ruler of rulers, protector of protectors.

You are the sovereign Lord,
Manifest in all forms
Yet yourself unmanifest.
You are everywhere
Yet the senses cannot find you.
You are the truth of Truth,
Not to be understood,
Never to be destroyed,
All-pervading,
Without form and hidden.
Lord and Light of the universe,
Save us from harm.

On you alone we meditate, who are One,
To you alone we offer our worship, who are One,
To you alone we bow down,
Sole Witness of all that seems,
In you alone we take refuge, who are One,
In you alone is our support, for ever and ever,
In you, Lord of this universe,
Life of all that lives,
Ship of our safety on life's sea.

I bow down to you, supreme Brahman,
I bow down to you, Atman supreme,
To you I bow down, who are beyond all forms and changes,
I bow down to you, the Ever-Living, again and again.[1]

                              [III. 50; 59-63; 74]

The Lord of this universe becomes pleased with him who is engaged in doing good to the world, since the Lord is its soul and refuge.

He is one. He ever is. He is the Truth, one without a second. He is the supreme Being. He is self-effulgent, ever shining. He is eternal consciousness and bliss.

He is unchangeable, self-existent, and serene, and he is beyond all predicates. He is the witness of all, the Self of all, pervading everything; he is the omnipresent.

He, the eternal, dwells concealed in the heart of all beings. Though himself devoid of senses, he is the illuminator of all the senses, the source of their powers.

He knows all, but none knows him. The world of forms appears real because he, the ground of all existence, is real.   [II. 33-38]

Through fear of him the wind blows, the sun gives heat, the clouds shower rain, and the trees in the forest flower.   [II. 44]

All gods and goddesses—nay, the whole universe from Brahma to a blade of grass—are his forms. If he be pleased, the universe is pleased.

Just as the pouring of water at its root nourishes the branches and leaves of a tree, so by worshipping him all the gods and goddesses attain bliss.   [II. 46-48]

As all rivers must go to the ocean, so all acts of worship reach him as the ultimate goal.   [II. 50]

For the attainment of liberation with ease and delight, there is no way but to worship him, to meditate upon him, and to pray to him.[2]   [II. 52]

From *Kularnava Tantra*

For one who bears the body, it is not possible to give up all activity. He who abandons the fruit of action, truly renounces. [IX. 125]

Ananda [Bliss] is the form of Brahman and that Ananda is installed in the body.   [V. 80]

The body itself is the temple; the jiva [individual soul] is God Sadashiva [Brahman].   [IX. 42]

Human birth, the ladder to liberation, is difficult to obtain. Who is more to be pitied than he who gets this birth and yet does not save himself?   [I. 16]

There is no mantra [sacred name of God] higher than meditation; no god higher than the Self; no worship higher than inner pursuit; there is no fruit greater than contentment.   [IX. 37]

When tired by Japa [chanting the name of the Lord], take to Dhyana [meditation]; tired in Dhyana, take again to Japa. Of him who does both Japa and Dhyana, the Mantra achieves most. [XV. 115]

Of him who is founded in the soul consciousness of the Self every movement is worship, each utterance is verily a Mantra, each gaze is meditation.³   [IX. 22]

NOTES

1. Translated by Swami Prabhavananda and Christopher Isherwood in Swami Prabhavananda and Clive Johnson, editors, *Prayers and Meditations Compiled from the Scriptures of India* (1967).
2. Translated by Swami Prabhavananda and Frederick Manchester in Swami Prabhavananda, *The Spiritual Heritage of India* (1964).
3. From M. P. Pandit, *Gems from the Tantras (Kularnava)* (First Series, 1969).

9. Vedanta Sutras of Badarayana

The *Vedanta Sutras,* along with the Upanishads and the Gita, are considered to be the most authoritative of Indian scriptures. Written sometime between the fifth and second centuries B.C. by the sage Badarayana, the *Vedanta Sutras* (also called the *Brahma Sutras*) expound the philosophy of the Upanishads in a series of terse, penetrating, and, at times, exceedingly obscure statements. Because of this latter characteristic, it is almost imperative that commentaries on the *Sutras* accompany their study. By far the most famous commentator on the *Vedanta Sutras* is Shankara, the eighth-century philosopher-seer, whose name has almost become synonymous with the school of Vedanta or nondualism. (See section 14.)

The *Sutras* are divided into four chapters. The first chapter deals with Brahman and its relation to the world and man, where an attempt is made to reconcile the various passages in the Vedas on the subject. The second chapter meets the objections to the view of Brahman, the soul, and the world expounded in the first, and exposes the errors of the rival theories. In chapter three the methods by which one can attain the knowledge of Brahman are examined, as well as the question of rebirth for those who fail to attain Brahman. The last chapter discusses the final result of Knowledge—liberation (*moksha*)—and the two paths possible after death (if one fails to attain liberation)—return (rebirth) and nonreturn (gradual liberation).

The selection given here is from Shankara's introductory commentary, clearly demonstrating his powers of reason and convincing logic to prove his theory of superimposition. In his commentary on the first sutra, he establishes prerequisites for the attainment of Knowledge.

The short selection by Ramanuja (A.D. 1017-1137) on meditation is from his commentary on the *Sutras*. Ramanuja was the well-known propounder of the school of qualified nondualistic Vedanta.

Vedanta Sutras of Badarayana

Shankara's Introduction

It is a matter not requiring any proof that the object and the subject,[1] whose respective spheres are the notion of the Thou (the Non-Ego)[2] and the Ego, and which are opposed to each other as much as darkness and light are, cannot be identified [i.e., the same]. All the less can their respective attributes be identified. Hence it follows that it is wrong to superimpose upon the subject—whose Self is intelligence, and which has for its sphere the notion of the Ego—the object whose sphere is the notion of the Non-Ego, and the attributes of the object, and vice versa, to superimpose the subject and the attributes of the subject on the object.

In spite of this, it is on the part of man a natural procedure—which has its cause in wrong knowledge—not to distinguish subject and object and their respective attributes, although they are absolutely distinct, but to superimpose upon each the characteristic nature and the attributes of the other, and thus, coupling the Real and the unreal,[3] to make use of expressions such as "That am I," "That is mine."[4] But what have we to understand by the term "superimposition"?—The apparent presentation, in the form of remembrance, to consciousness of something previously observed, in some other thing. . . . But how is it possible that on the Interior Self [Atman], which itself is not an object, there should be superimposed objects and their attributes? For every one superimposes an object only on such other objects as are placed before him (i.e., in contact with his sense organs), and you[5] have said before that the interior Self which is entirely disconnected from the idea of the Thou (the Non-Ego) is never an object.

It is not, we reply, non-object in the absolute sense. For it is the object of the notion of the Ego,[6] and the interior Self is well known to exist on account of its immediate (intuitive) presentation. Nor is it an exceptionless rule that objects can be superimposed only on such other objects as are before us—that is, in contact with our sense organs. For nondiscerning men superimpose on the ether, which is not an object of perception, a dark-blue color.

Hence it follows that the assumption of the Non-Self being superimposed on the interior Self is not unreasonable. . . . (The superimposition of the Non-Self will be understood more definitely from the following examples.) Extra-personal attributes are superimposed on the Self if a man considers himself sound and entire, or the contrary, as long as his wife, children, and so on are sound and entire or not. Attributes of the body are superimposed on the Self if a man thinks of himself (his Self) as stout, lean, fair; as standing, walking, or jumping. Attributes of the sense organs if he thinks "I am mute, or deaf, or one-eyed, or blind." Attributes of the internal organ [the ego] when he considers himself subject to desire, intention, doubt, determination, and so on.

Thus the producer of the notion of the Ego is superimposed on the interior Self, which, in reality, is the witness of all the modifications of the internal organ; and, vice-versa, the interior Self, which is the witness of everything, is superimposed on the internal organ, senses, and so on. In this way, there [continues on] . . . this endless superimposition, which appears in the form of wrong conception, is the cause of individual souls appearing as agents and enjoyers (of the results of their actions) and is observed by every one.

With a view to freeing one's self from that wrong notion, which is the cause of all evil, and thereby attaining the knowledge of the absolute unity of the Self, the study of the Vedanta-texts is begun. . . .

1. *Then therefore [let us begin] the enquiry into Brahman.*

. . . [The word "then" implies that] something should be stated subsequent to which the enquiry into Brahman is proposed. Well, then, we maintain that the antecedent conditions are: [1] the discrimination [between] what is eternal and what is noneternal; [2] the renunciation of all desire to enjoy the fruit (of one's ac-

tions) both here and hereafter; [3] the acquirement of tranquility, self-restraint, and the other means;[7] and [4] the desire for final release [liberation]. . . .
The word "therefore" intimates a reason. Because the Veda . . . teaches that the highest aim of man is realized by the knowledge of Brahman;[8] therefore, the enquiry into Brahman is to be undertaken subsequently to the acquirement of the mentioned means.[9]

[*Ramanuja, the twelfth-century exponent of qualified nondualism, also wrote a commentary on the* Vedanta Sutras. *The selection below, translated by Swami Vivekananda, is a discussion of meditation from Ramanuja's commentary on the first aphorism.*—Ed.]

Meditation is a constant remembering [of the thing meditated upon], which flows like oil poured from one vessel to another. When this kind of remembering has been attained [in relation to God] all bonds break. Thus the scriptures speak of constant recollectedness as a means to liberation. This remembering again is the same as seeing, because it has the same significance, as is evident from the passage, "When He who is far away and near is seen, the bonds of the heart are broken, all doubts vanish, and all effects of karma disappear." He who is near can be seen, but he who is far away can only be remembered. Nevertheless the scriptures say that we have to see Him who is near as well as far away, thereby indicating to us that the above kind of remembering is as good as seeing. This remembrance when exalted assumes the same form as seeing. . . . Worship is constant remembering, as may be seen from the principal texts of the scriptures. Knowing, which is the same as repeated worship, has been described as constant remembering. . . . Thus the memory, which has attained to the level of direct perception, is spoken of in the Shruti [scripture] as a means of liberation. "This Atman is not to be reached through various sciences, nor by intellect, nor by much study of the Vedas. Whomsoever this Atman desires, by him is the Atman attained; unto him this Atman reveals himself." Here, after saying that mere hearing, thinking, and meditating are not the means of attaining this Atman, the passage continues—"Whomsoever this Atman desires, by him the Atman is attained." The extremely beloved is desired; he by whom this Atman is extremely beloved becomes the most beloved of the Atman. So that this beloved may attain the Atman, the Lord himself helps. For it has been said by the Lord: "Those who are constantly attached to Me and worship Me with love—I give that direction to their will by which they come to Me." Therefore it is said, to whomsoever this remembering, which is the same as direct perception, is very dear, because it is dear to the object of such memory-perception, he is desired by the Supreme Atman, by him the Supreme Atman is attained. This constant remembrance is denoted by the word bhakti (love).[10]

NOTES

1. The subject is the Universal Self whose nature is intelligence (chit); the object comprises whatever is of non-intelligent nature, viz. bodies with their sense organs, internal organs, and the objects of the senses, i.e., the external material world. [Translator]

2. The object is said to have for its sphere the notion of the "thou," not the notion of the "this" or "that," in order better to mark its absolute opposition to the subject or Ego. [Translator]

3. The Atman or real Self (the Real) and the body, sense objects, and so forth (unreal, i.e., the non-Self). [Ed.]

4. "The body, etc. is my Self; sickness, death, children, wealth, and so forth belong to my Self." [Translator]

5. In his commentary, Shankara has employed the rough structure of a dialogue between himself and a group of hypothetical opponents. In this sentence, "you" obviously refers to Shankara. [Ed.]

6. The real Self is in reality non-object, for it is self-luminous, i.e., the subjective factor in all cognition. But it becomes the object of the idea of Ego in so far as it is limited, conditioned by its adjuncts, which are the product of ignorance. [Ed.]

7. These "other means" which together are popularly known as the six treasures of virtue are: mental poise (uparati), forbearance (titiksha), self-surrender (samadhana), and faith (shraddha). [Ed.]

8. "He who knows Brahman attains the highest." Taittiriya Upan., II, 1. [Translator]

9. From George Thibaut, translator, The Vedanta Sutras of Badarayana, Part I (1962 edition).

10. From Swami Vivekananda, Complete Works, Vol. III, 8th ed. (1960).

10. Bhakti Sutras of Narada

The *Bhakti Sutras* are a connected series of eighty-four aphorisms composed by the ancient sage Narada on the philosophy of *bhakti* or love of God. When the *Sutras* are closely studied, they are found to be not only a progressive means to the attainment of divine love, but a concise record of Narada's own spiritual life and mystical experiences. "The best path to union with God," said Sri Ramakrishna, the nineteenth-century Bengali saint, "is to follow the way of divine love as expounded by Narada." According to Narada, the culminating spiritual virtue is the total surrender of the self to God; it is the remedy of all ills and the source of all wisdom.

Who was Narada? We discover his name for the first time in the *Chandogya Upanishad* as a young man approaching the sage Sanatkumar for instruction. We next find him in the *Bhagavata Purana* as an illumined soul. He was unquestionably one of the great gurus or spiritual teachers of all time.

In the following selection, the translator has provided a full and enlightening commentary on Narada's opening sutras, which define bhakti.

Bhakti Sutras of Narada

2. *Bhakti is intense love for God.*

Narada does not use the word God, but the indefinite neuter pronoun *this*—and is translating the aphorism into English I have altered it, because "intense love for this" would not mean anything to the reader.

It is interesting to consider why Narada used the pronoun "this," instead of God or Brahman, or Atman, or Rama, or Krishna or some other divine name.

One reason is that he wished his teachings to be completely

nonsectarian. The use of the pronoun *this* in contrast to *that* suggests that the Reality, no matter by what name it may be called, is nearer than the nearest—the innermost Self of our being; and is to be found within the sanctuary of our own hearts and in the hearts of all beings.

As already stated, God (I use the word God to denote the ultimate Reality—there being no other word in English to substitute for it) is to be experienced with the opening of divine sight.

Narada avoids defining God anywhere in this treatise, because to define is to limit God. Furthermore, when a man experiences God, he is unable to express Him in terms of relative experience. To quote the words of Sri Ramakrishna: "When one attains *samadhi* then alone comes the knowledge of Brahman. In that realization all thoughts cease, one becomes perfectly silent. There is no power of speech left by which to express Brahman."

But again we find that the great sages and seers have tried to express the truth of God in varied ways. Some say he is personal, and others impersonal. Some say he is with form and others without form. Some say he is endowed with divine attributes, others say he is attributeless. . . .

The various ideals of God which devotees worship according to their spiritual tendencies or inclinations may be the Personal God with attributes, under the aspects of Vishnu, Shiva, Kali, Jehovah, Allah and so forth, or incarnations of God, such as Rama, Krishna, Buddha, Christ, or Ramakrishna.

Narada defines *bhakti* as "intense love" for God. This intense love that the sage speaks of refers to the love that arises in the heart of a devotee who has the vision of God, when he has become a God-drunken lover. That this maddening love is the same as experiencing God-consciousness is evident also from Narada's descriptions of the nature of this love in the aphorisms which follow.

One day, while Swami Vivekananda was holding classes for a few intimate disciples at Thousand Island Park, he took up the study of the Bhakti Sutras. As Swamiji translated this particular aphorism, he commented upon it by quoting the following words of his Master, Sri Ramakrishna: "This world is a huge lunatic asylum where all men are mad—some after money, some after women, some after name or fame, and a few after God. God is the philosopher's stone that turns us to gold in an instant: the form remains, but the nature is changed; the human form remains, but no more can we do harm or commit any sin.

"Thinking of God, some weep, some sing, some dance, some say wonderful things—but all speak of nothing but God."

This maddening intense love arises only when we feel his love for us; this is tangibly felt when we experience ecstasy in God-vision.

My Master, Swami Brahmananda, once told me, "Our love is so deep that we do not let you know how much we love you." Indeed this is the same kind of deep love that God has for us—for all beings. And in order that we may feel that love of his by going into ecstasy, we need to practice spiritual disciplines, ". . . to know the love of Christ, which passeth knowledge, that ye might be filled with all the fulness of God." [Eph. 3:19] . . .

Before, however, I try to explain what is meant by this intense love, let me point out that a *bhakta,* following the path of devotion, begins by worshiping God as a Personal Being. Personal Being, as already pointed out, may have various aspects, such as Vishnu, Shiva, Kali, Jehovah, and so forth.

But perhaps for the Western devotee (also for the devotees in India) it will be easier to grasp or understand the worship of an avatar, or divine Incarnation—Krishna or Christ, Buddha or Rama-krishna.

Of course, according to the Vedantic tradition, there is not only one avatar. It is, rather, the one God who incarnates himself in different ages, in different forms and under different names. To quote the *Bhagavad-Gita* (Song of God), Sri Krishna says:

> When goodness grows weak,
> When evil increases,
> I make myself a body.
> In every age I come back
> To deliver the holy,
> To destroy the sin of the sinner
> To establish righteousness.

This intense love is a transcendental experience of bliss, inexpressible. The ego is completely lost.

Before I give some illustrations from the saints and seers who attained complete union with the Lord, realizing him to be the

Self, the true being, within themselves, let me describe the main characteristics of divine love:

First, a true devotee loves the Lord for love's sake. There is no bargaining or shopkeeping in his love. He does not even seek liberation, though, in spite of himself, he becomes liberated.

Another characteristic of divine love is that it knows no fear. Swami Vivekananda said that to worship God through fear of punishment, because of human weaknesses, is degrading religion. Sri Sarada Devi once said that if a baby plays in mud puddles and gets itself dirty, does the mother throw away the baby? Or does she pick him up, wash him, and then take him on her lap? God is more than our own father or mother. He, alone, is love itself. My Master, Swami Brahmananda, once told me, "Is there any sin in God's eye? A glance from him burns away all sins like a match put to a heap of cotton."

Lastly, this love knows no rival. To a devotee, God is the one and only beloved. Sri Chaitanya says in his prayer to the Lord:

O Thou, who stealest the hearts of Thy devotees,
Do with me what Thou wilt—
For Thou art my heart's Beloved, Thou and Thou alone.

3. *In its intrinsic nature this divine love is immortal bliss.*

What is the true nature of this immortal bliss? It is a state of absolute felicity and beatitude. My Master once told me, "People talk of enjoying life; but what do those who are steeped in worldliness and passions know of the joy of life? They alone who devote themselves to God and find sweetness in Him begin to taste the true joy of life." There is a word in Sanskrit *Madhava,* the sweet one, which is one of the names of the Lord.

In the *Taittiriya Upanishad* we read, "The Self-Existent is the essence of felicity. Who could live, who could breathe, if that blissful Self dwelt not within the lotus of the heart? He it is that gives joy." We find in the *Svetasvatara Upanishad:* "As a soiled piece of metal, when it has been cleaned, shines brightly, so the dweller in the body, when he has realized the truth of the Self, is freed from sorrow and attains to bliss."

A similar truth is to be discovered in the Bible: "Therefore the redeemed of the Lord shall return, and come with singing unto Zion; and everlasting joy shall be upon their head: they shall

obtain gladness and joy; and sorrow and mourning shall flee away."
[Isa. 51:11] Says Jesus: "Enter thou into the joy of thy Lord."
[Matt. 25:21]. . . .

Any happiness or pleasure that a man may derive from obtaining the objects of his desire in the world of the senses is the effect of some cause, and as such is ephemeral and finite. It is true that a man has to undergo spiritual disciplines and make efforts to find God. But these disciplines and efforts are undertaken in order to feel the divine Grace; and when that Grace is felt, then a man knows that his own efforts would have been impossible without the Grace of the Lord.

My Master often said, "God is not a commodity that you can buy. It is only through His grace that man finds the bliss of attainment of God." . . .

5. *On attaining that a man does not desire anything else, he grieves no more; is free from hatred or jealousy; he does not take pleasure in the vanities of life; and he loses all eagerness to gain anything for himself.*

Let us examine the meaning of each of the parts of this aphorism:

On attaining that a man does not desire anything else. Shankara says: "The fruit of illumination is the stilling of desire; the fruit of stilled desire is experience of the bliss of the Atman, whence follows peace."

Desire arises from a sense of limitation and imperfection. A man of attainment feels no lack, what else is there for him to desire? There are two words in Sanskrit—*nishkama,* which means "desirelessness," and *purnakama,* which means "complete fulfillment of all desires." A man of God is purnakama, because in him there is a complete fulfillment. There is nothing more to gain or achieve. As it is said in the *Bhagavad-Gita:* "Then he knows that infinite happiness which can be realized by the purified heart but is beyond the grasp of the senses. He stands firm in that realization. Because of it, he can never again wander from the inmost truth of his being." And later:

> Now that he holds it
> He knows this treasure
> Above all others.

But there is a difference between a spiritual aspirant and a man of attainment. To quote the *Bhagavad-Gita* again:

> The abstinent run away from what they desire
> But carry their desires with them;
> When a man enters Reality,
> He leaves his desires behind him.

But there is one desire left in him. And that is to serve God in mankind. An illumined soul's heart melts in sympathy with the sufferings of others. His heart becomes full of compassion. . . .

Truly has it been said in the *Bhagavad-Gita:*

> Who burns with the bliss
> And suffers the sorrow
> Of every creature
> Within his own heart,
> Making his own
> Each bliss and each sorrow:
> Him I hold highest
> Of all the Yogis.

He grieves no more: Only "he suffers the sorrow of every creature." He is . . . *free from hatred and jealousy.* Jealousy or hatred arise from unfulfilled desire. How can jealousy or hatred exist in a man who sees his Beloved everywhere? My Master once said to me, "I see one God wearing many masks—the mask of a saint or a sinner."

But supposing someone hurts or insults a holy man? How would he react? The best illustration of that is given in the Song of the Mendicant in the *Srimad Bhagavatam.* The mendicant was badly hurt and insulted by some ignorant people. And he walked on, saying to himself, "Even if thou dost think another person is causing thee happiness or misery, thou art really neither happy nor wretched, for thou art the Atman, the changeless spirit; thy sense of happiness and misery is due to a false identification of thy Self with the body which alone is subject to change. Thy Self is the real Self in all. With whom shouldst thou be angry for causing pain if accidentally thou dost bite thy tongue with thy teeth?"

He does not take pleasure in the vanities of life. His heart is in Brahman, the eternal treasure, and in whom is abiding bliss. So naturally he cannot give his heart to pleasures that are only fleeting. The fleeting pleasures of life are only the shadows of that blissful Consciousness of Brahman.

As Plotinus says: "There are no more two, but one; the soul is no more conscious of the body and mind, but knows that she has what she desired, and that she is where no deception can come, and she would not exchange that bliss for all the heaven of heavens."

He loses all eagerness to gain anything for himself. This does not mean however that he becomes inert and does not act. It is true that as Sri Krishna says in the *Bhagavad-Gita:* "But when a man has found delight and satisfaction and peace in the Atman, then he is no longer obliged to perform any kind of action. He has nothing to gain in the world by action, and nothing to lose by refraining from action." However, Sri Krishna urges his disciple to act, saying, "Your motive in working should be to set others, by your example, on the path of duty." He continues:

> The ignorant work
> For the fruit of their action:
> The wise must work also
> Without desire
> Pointing man's feet
> To the path of duty.

> Let them show by example
> How work is holy
> When the heart of the worker
> Is fixed on the Highest.

There is another meaning to the last sentence in this aphorism: he does not exert himself. That is to say, he does not act by his own will. He has completely surrendered his will to the will of the Lord. As Tennyson said:

> Our wills are ours, we know not how,
> Our wills are ours to make them thine.[1]

NOTE

1. From Swami Prabhavananda, translator and commentator, *The Way of Divine Love as Taught by Narada* (unpublished).

11. Yoga Sutras of Patanjali

According to Patanjali, as well as other Indian schools of thought, the practice of religion consists in developing man's supersensuous power in order to attain freedom from the bonds of birth and death. The ways to attain this liberation are mentioned in the Vedas, Upanishads, and other early works; in fact, all of these scriptures discuss the means by which we can unfold the divinity within and thereby attain *moksha* (liberation). Patanjali restated and reformulated this doctrine in a systematic manner which could be easily followed by all spiritual aspirants. Thus the *Sutras* provide a step-by-step means by which transcendental consciousness can be reached and liberation attained. Patanjali cannot be considered the founder of yoga, but rather the first to gather together the spiritual precepts and practices known to the yogis and build them into a system.

What is yoga? It can literally be translated "union," and in this primary sense it means to yoke oneself to the true Self or God; in a secondary sense, it refers to the methods for achieving that union. In his second sutra, Patanjali states that this union is brought about by the "control of the thought waves of the mind." The word "yoga" has unfortunately been too often identified in the West with the practice of *hatha yoga,* which mainly emphasizes postures and physical exercises. Patanjali, however, is primarily concerned with controlling the mind, for only in this way can liberation be attained.

Patanjali's yoga is also known as *raja yoga,* which contains the universal principles of meditation—a discipline common to the other paths or yogas as well.

Yoga Sutras of Patanjali

I. *Yoga and Its Aims*[1]

1. *This is the beginning of instruction in yoga.*
Basically, *yoga* means "union." It is the Sanskrit ancestor of the

English word "yoke." Hence, it comes to mean a method of spiritual union. A yoga is a method—any one of many—by which an individual may become united with the Godhead, the Reality which underlies this apparent, ephemeral universe. To achieve such union is to reach the state of perfect yoga. Christianity has a corresponding term, "the mystic union," which expresses a similar idea.

Bhoja, one of the classical commentators on these aphorisms, defines Patanjali's use of the word yoga as "an effort to separate the Atman (the Reality) from the non-Atman (the apparent)."

One who practices yoga is called a *yogi*.

2. *Yoga is the control of thought-waves in the mind.*

According to Patanjali, the mind (*chitta*) is made up of three components, *manas, buddhi*, and *ahamkar*. Manas is the recording faculty which receives impressions gathered by the senses from the outside world. Buddhi is the discriminative faculty which classifies these impressions and reacts to them. Ahamkar is the ego-sense which claims these impressions for its own and stores them up as individual knowledge. For example, manas reports: "A large animate object is quickly approaching." Buddhi decides: "That's a bull. It is angry. It wants to attack someone." Ahamkar screams: "It wants to attack *me*, Patanjali. It is *I* who see this bull. It is *I* who am frightened. It is *I* who am about to run away." Later, from the branches of a nearby tree, ahamkar may add: "Now *I* know that this bull (which is not *I*) is dangerous. There are others who do not know this; it is *my* own personal knowledge, which will cause *me* to avoid this bull in future."

God, the underlying Reality, is by definition omnipresent. If the Reality exists at all, it must be everywhere; it must be present within every sentient being, every inanimate object. God-within-the-creature is known in the Sanskrit language as the *Atman* or *Purusha*, the real Self. Patanjali speaks always of the Purusha (which means literally "the Godhead that dwells within the body"), but we shall substitute Atman throughout this translation, because Atman is the word used in the Upanishads and the *Bhagavad-Gita*, and students are therefore likely to be more accustomed to it. According to the Upanishads and the Gita, the one Atman is present within all creatures. Patanjali, following Sankhya philosophy, believed that each individual creature and object has its separate, but identical,

Purusha. This philosophical point of difference has no practical importance for the spiritual aspirant.

The mind seems to be intelligent and conscious. Yoga philosophy teaches that it is not. It has only a borrowed intelligence. The Atman is intelligence itself, is pure consciousness. The mind merely reflects that consciousness and so appears to be conscious.

Knowledge or perception is a thought-wave (*vritti*) in the mind. All knowledge is therefore objective. Even what Western psychologists call introspection or self-knowledge is objective knowledge according to Patanjali, since the mind is not the seer, but only an instrument of knowledge, an object of perception like the outside world. The Atman, the real seer, remains unknown.

Every perception arouses the ego-sense, which says: "I know this." But this is the ego speaking, not the Atman, the real Self. The ego-sense is caused by the identification of the Atman with the mind, senses, etc. It is as if a little electric light bulb would declare: "I am the electric current" and then proceed to describe electricity as a pear-shaped glass object containing filaments of wire. Such identification is absurd—as absurd as the ego's claim to be the real Self. Nevertheless, the electric current *is* present in the light bulb, and the Atman is in all things, everywhere.

When an event or object in the external world is recorded by the senses, a thought-wave is raised in the mind. The ego-sense identifies itself with this wave. If the thought-wave is pleasant, the ego-sense feels, "I am happy"; if the wave is unpleasant, "I am unhappy." This false identification is the cause of all our misery— for even the ego's temporary sensation of happiness brings anxiety, a desire to cling to the object of pleasure, and this prepares future possibilities of becoming unhappy. The real Self, the Atman, remains forever outside the power of thought-waves, it is eternally pure, enlightened and free—the only true, unchanging happiness. It follows, therefore, that man can never know his real Self as long as the thought-waves and the ego-sense are being identified. In order to become enlightened we must bring the thought-waves under control, so that this false identification may cease. The Gita teaches us that "Yoga is the breaking of contact with pain."

Describing the action of the thought-waves, the commentators employ a simple image—the image of a lake. If the surface of a lake is lashed into waves, the water becomes muddy and the bottom cannot be seen. The lake represents the mind and the bottom of the lake the Atman.

When Patanjali speaks of "control of thought-waves," he does not refer to a momentary or superficial control. Many people believe that the practice of yoga is concerned with "making your mind a blank"—a condition which could, if it were really desirable, be much more easily achieved by asking a friend to hit you over the head with a hammer. No spiritual advantage is ever gained by self-violence. We are not trying to check the thought-waves by smashing the organs which record them. We have to do something much more difficult—to unlearn the false identification of the thought-waves with the ego-sense. This process of unlearning involves a complete transformation of character, a "renewal of the mind," as St. Paul puts it.

15. *Non-attachment is self-mastery; it is freedom from desire for what is seen or heard.*

The waves of the mind can be made to flow in two opposite directions—either toward the objective world ("the will to desire") or toward true self-knowledge ("the will to liberation"). Therefore both practice and non-attachment are necessary. Indeed, it is useless and even dangerous to attempt one without the other. If we try to practice spiritual disciplines without attempting to control the thought-waves of desire, our minds will become violently agitated and perhaps permanently unbalanced. If we attempt nothing more than a rigid negative control of the waves of desire, without raising waves of love, compassion and devotion to oppose them, then the result may be even more tragic. This is why certain strict puritans suddenly and mysteriously commit suicide. They make a cold, stern effort to be "good"—that is, not to think "bad" thoughts —and when they fail, as all human beings sometimes must, they cannot face this humiliation, which is really nothing but hurt pride, and the emptiness inside themselves. In the Taoist scriptures we read: "Heaven arms with compassion those whom it would not see destroyed."

The spiritual disciplines which we are to practice will be described in due course. They are known as the eight "limbs" of yoga. Perseverance is very important, in this connection. No temporary failure, however disgraceful or humiliating, should ever be used as an excuse for giving up the struggle. If we are learning to ski, we are not ashamed when we fall down, or find ourselves lying in some ridiculous entangled position. We pick ourselves up and start again. Never mind if people laugh, or sneer at us. Unless we are hypocrites we shall not care what impression we make upon the onlookers. No failure is ever really a failure unless we stop trying altogether—indeed, it may be a blessing in disguise, a much-needed lesson.

Non-attachment is the exercise of discrimination. We gradually gain control of the "painful" or impure thought-waves by asking ourselves: "Why do I really desire that object? What permanent advantage should I gain by possessing it? In what way would its possession help me toward greater knowledge and freedom?" The answers to these questions are always disconcerting. They show us that the desired object is not only useless as a means to liberation but potentially harmful as a means to ignorance and bondage; and, further, that our desire is not really desire for the object-in-itself at all, but only a desire to desire something, a mere restlessness in the mind.

It is fairly easy to reason all this out in a calm moment. But our non-attachment is put to the test when the mind is suddenly swept by a huge wave of anger or lust or greed. Then it is only by a determined effort of will that we can remember what our reason already knows—that this wave, and the sense-object which raised it, and the ego-sense which identifies the experience with itself, are all alike transient and superficial—that they are not the underlying Reality.

II. *Yoga and Its Practice*

28. *As soon as all impurities have been removed by the practice of spiritual disciplines—the "limbs" of yoga—a man's spiritual vision opens to the light-giving knowledge of the Atman.*

29. *The eight limbs of yoga are: the various forms of abstention from evil-doing (yama), the various observances (niyamas), posture (asana), control of the prana (pranayama) [vital energy], withdrawal of the mind from sense objects (pratyahara), concentration (dharana), meditation (dhyana) and absorption in the Atman (samadhi).*

30. *Yama is abstention from harming others, from falsehood, from theft, from incontinence, and from greed.*

Abstention from harming others is living and acting in such a way as never to cause any pain to a living soul by one's thought, word, or deed. . . .

Abstention from falsehood is truthfulness in thought, word, and deed. In the Gita we are admonished "to speak without ever causing pain to another, to be truthful, and to say always what is kind and beneficial." . . .

Abstention from theft has a deeper significance than what the phrase literally means. We must realize that nothing belongs to us; consequently, we may not harbor the idea of possession or own attachment to things of this world. . . .

Abstention from incontinence is chastity in thought, word, and deed. . . . Such energy is indispensable to a religious teacher. With it comes tremendous force and gigantic will to turn humanity onto the path of good.

31. *These forms of abstention are basic rules of conduct. They must be practiced wthout any reservations as to time, place, purpose, or caste rules.*

Patanjali admits of no excuses or exceptions. When he tells us, for example, to abstain from harming others he means exactly what he says. He would have no patience with a man who assured him: "Certainly I'll abstain from killing—except, of course, in time of war, on a battlefield, when we're fighting in a just cause and it's my duty anyway, as a member of the armed forces."

32. *The niyamas [observances] are purity, contentment, mortification, study and devotion to God.*

Purity is cleanliness, both physical and mental. Just as a regular habit of bathing is formed for physical cleanliness, in the same way a regular habit is to be formed of bathing our inner organ, the mind, by feeling within it the living presence of God. . . .

Contentment is the practice of quiet acceptance of whatever comes in the course of our lives, and the maintenance of inner poise. . . .

The Sanskrit word used by Patanjali in this aphorism is *tapas* [for mortification], which means, in its primary sense, that which generates heat or energy. Tapas is the practice of conserving energy and directing it toward the goal of yoga, toward union with the Atman. . . .

Austerity for austerity's sake easily degenerates into a perverse cult of self-torture; and this is another danger—that the end should be forgotten in an exaggerated cultivation of the means. . . . True austerity, in the Hindu understanding of the word, is not a process of fanatical self-punishment but of quiet and sane self-control. . . .

Study, . . . means study of the scriptures and of other sacred books which deal with the spiritual life. It also refers to the practice of japam, the repetition of the name of God.

46. *Posture (asana) is to be seated in a position which is firm but relaxed.*

Asana means two things: the place on which the yogi sits, and the manner in which he sits there. Thus, we read in the *Vedanta Sutras* (IV. i): "Worship is possible in a sitting posture, because this encourages meditation. The meditating person is compared to the immovable earth. There is no law of place; wherever the mind is concentrated, there worship should be performed."

49. *After mastering posture, one must practice control of the prana (pranayama) by stopping the motions of inhalation and exhalation.*

Pranayama means control of vital energy, or of the life-principle. Just what the life-principle really is, no one can tell, but we do recognize its expression. It is the energy that enables us to act, to think, to breathe. Pranayama is control of this energy, and the word has come to be associated with breathing exercises based on a principle somewhat analogous to that propounded by William James to the Western world. The principle may be stated thus: The mind and the body are closely related, and act and react upon each other; emotions cause characteristic changes in the body, and changes in the body evoke corresponding emotions in the mind. On this principle of experimental psychology, discovered in the West in recent years, but known to the yogis of India from almost a beginningless past, there is taught control of the breath to bring calmness and concentration to the mind. The state of the mind, whether it be lethargic or restless or calm, is first observed in the breathing, for the rise of passions brings about characteristic changes in the way we breathe. If, then, breathing can be made rhythmic, calm is the inevitable result. If, moreover, the mind is in process of concentration, we scarcely breathe, and when the mind is in a state of complete concentration, we do not breathe at all. Pranayama needs therefore to be practised first in order to win control over the body and mind, and finally to control the very life energy itself.[2] (It must be emphasized, however, that breathing exercises should not be undertaken without the supervision of an expert teacher.)

54. *When the mind is withdrawn from sense-objects, the sense-organs also withdraw themselves from their respective objects and thus are said to imitate the mind. This is known as pratyahara.*

55. *Thence arises complete mastery over the senses.*

Just as the provinces of a country are controlled by first taking over the central government, so we must begin by controlling the mind before we can control the rest of the body. As long as there is desire in the mind, the sense-organs will move eagerly and almost involuntarily toward the objects of desire. A man is aptly said to have a "roving eye" when his eyes, of their own accord, follow the figure of an attractive girl passing him in the street. The sense-organs are like animals which instinctively imitate their master. If the master is weak and subject to certain passions, then the sense-organs will imitate and even exaggerate his weakness, dragging him along after them as a child is dragged by a strong, unruly dog. But when the mind is strong and self-controlled the sense-organs become its orderly and obedient servants. They imitate its strength instead of its weakness. Every movement of the body expresses the self-control of the mind.

III. *Powers*

1. *Concentration (dharana) is holding the mind within a center of spiritual consciousness in the body, or fixing it on some divine form, either within the body or outside it.*

Through the practice of concentration, the mind eventually reaches a stage when it ceases all fluctuation.

In order to concentrate, you must first fix your mind upon the Inner Light within one of these lotuses [one of the spiritual centers or *chakras*] as your teacher directs. Or you may concentrate upon the form of your Chosen Ideal, trying to visualize that form either within a lotus or outside your own body altogether.

2. *Meditation (dhyana) is an unbroken flow of thought toward the object of concentration.*

In other words, meditation is prolonged concentration. The process of meditation is often compared to the pouring of oil from one vessel to another, in a steady, unbroken stream. We have seen (I, 2) that Patanjali defines thought as a wave (vritti) in the mind. Ordinarily a thought-wave arises, remains in the mind for a moment, and then subsides, to be succeeded by another wave. In the practice of meditation, a succession of identical waves are raised in the mind; and this is done so quickly that no one wave is allowed to subside before another rises to take its place. The effect is therefore one of perfect continuity. If you shoot a hundred feet of film without moving your camera or your object, and then project the result on a screen, your audience might just as well be looking at a single still photograph. The many identical images are fused into one.

3. *When, in meditation, the true nature of the object shines forth, not distorted by the mind of the perceiver, that is absorption (samadhi).*

It is only in the supersensuous perception of samadhi that we see an object in the truth of its own nature, absolutely free from the distortions of our imagination. Samadhi is, in fact, much more than perception; it is direct knowledge. When Sri Ramakrishna told Vivekananda, "I see God more real than I see you," he was speaking the literal truth. For Ramakrishna meant that he saw God in samadhi, while he saw Vivekananda with the eyes of his ordinary sense-perception which must necessarily retain a measure of distortion.

NOTES

1. From Swami Prabhavananda and Christopher Isherwood, translators and commentators, *How to Know God: The Yoga Aphorisms of Patanjali* (1953), except where otherwise noted.

2. Above commentary in Swami Prabhavananda, *The Spiritual Heritage of India* (1964), p. 252.

12. The Laws of Manu

The Laws of Manu were most likely not the work of one man, but of several lawmakers over the centuries; thus we cannot ascribe any single date to their composition. But they are known to be exceedingly ancient. The Laws or *Dharma Shastras* are divided into twelve books which concern nearly every aspect of man's life on earth: education, marriage, domestic life, the organization of the caste system, punishments, and reincarnation. An account of creation is given, and rules for ethical behavior. Self-control, for instance, is strongly emphasized; the Hindu citizen was expected to control his lust and other passions in order to prepare himself for a life of *sannyasa* or renunciation once the duties of marriage and child-raising were past.

The purpose of the Laws is implicit: the preservation of a stable society, founded on fixed traditions, which seeks to conform the lower will to the higher—the will of the individual to the will of God. The Laws, therefore, have a divine purpose, and in this sense are highly respected as scripture rather than as a body of secular rules. Although the laws themselves have largely fallen into disuse, the principles behind them still have universal meaning and application.

The Laws of Manu

Studentship

88. A wise man should strive to restrain his organs which run wild among alluring sensual objects, like a charioteer his horses.

94. Desire is never extinguished by the enjoyment of desired objects; it only grows stronger like a fire fed with clarified butter.

95. If one man should obtain all those sensual enjoyments and another should renounce them all, the renunciation of all pleasure is far better than the attainment of them.

96. Those organs which are strongly attached to sensual pleasures, cannot so effectually be restrained by abstinence from enjoyments as by a constant pursuit of true knowledge.

97. Neither the study of the Vedas, nor liberality, nor sacrifices, nor any self-imposed restraint, nor austerities, [will] procure the attainment of rewards to a man whose heart is contaminated by sensuality.

98. That man may be considered to have really subdued his organs, who on hearing and touching and seeing, on tasting and smelling anything neither rejoices nor repines.

173. The student who has been initiated must be instructed in the performance of the vows, and gradually learn the Veda, observing the prescribed rules.

[Book II]

Household Life

1. Having dwelt with a teacher during the fourth part of a man's life, a Brahmana shall live during the second quarter of his existence in his house, after he has wedded a wife.

2. A Brahmana must seek a means of subsistence which either causes no, or at least little, pain to others, and live by that except in times of distress.

3. For the purpose of gaining bare subsistence, let him accumulate property by following those irreproachable occupations which are prescribed for his caste, without unduly fatiguing his body.

11. Let him never, for the sake of subsistence, follow the ways of the world; let him live the pure, straightforward, honest life of a Brahmana.

12. He who desires happiness must strive after a perfectly contented disposition and control himself; for happiness has contentment for its root, the root of unhappiness is the contrary disposition.

15. Whether he be rich or even in distress, let him not seek wealth through pursuits to which men cleave, nor by forbidden occupations, nor let him accept presents from any giver whosoever he may be.

16. Let him not, out of desire for enjoyments, attach himself to any sensual pleasures, and let him carefully obviate an excessive attachment to them, by reflecting on their worthlessness in his heart.

17. Let him avoid all means of acquiring wealth which impede the study of the Veda; let him maintain himself anyhow, but study, because that devotion . . . secures the realization of his aims.

[Book IV]

Lawful and Forbidden Food

56. There is no sin in eating meat, in drinking spirituous liquor, and in carnal intercourse, for that is the natural way of created beings, but abstention brings great rewards.

[Book V]

The Hermit in the Forest

1. A twice-born householder, who has lived according to the law in the order of householders, may, taking a firm resolution and keeping his organs in subjection, dwell in the forest, duly observing the rules given below.

2. When a householder sees his skin wrinkled, and his hair white, and the sons of his sons, then he may resort to the forest.

3. Abandoning all food raised by cultivation, and all his belongings, he may depart into the forest, either committing his wife to his sons, or accompanied by her.

4. Taking with him the sacred fire and the implements required for domestic sacrifices, he may go forth from the village into the forest and reside there, duly controlling his senses.

8. Let him be always industrious in privately reciting the Veda; let him be patient of hardships, friendly towards all, of collected mind, ever liberal and never a receiver of gifts, and compassionate towards all living creatures.

27. From Brahmanas who live as ascetics, let him receive alms, barely sufficient to support life, or from other householders of the twice-born castes who reside in the forest.

28. Or the hermit who dwells in the forest may bring food from a village, receiving it either in a hollow dish of leaves, in his naked hand, or in a broken earthen dish, and may eat eight mouthfuls.

29. These and other observances must a Brahmana who dwells in the forest diligently practise, and in order to attain complete union with the supreme Soul, he must study the various sacred texts contained in the Upanishads,

30. As well as those rites and texts which have been practised and studied by the sages, and by Brahmana householders, in order to increase their knowledge of Brahman, and their austerity, and in order to sanctify their bodies.

[Book VI]

The Ascetic

52. His hair, nails, and beard being clipped, carrying an alms-bowl, a staff, and a water-pot, let him continually wander about controlling himself and not hurting any creature.

54. A gourd, a wooden bowl, an earthen dish, or one made of split cane, Manu, the son of Svayambhu, has declared to be vessels suitable for an ascetic.

55. Let him go to beg once a day, let him not be eager to obtain a large quantity of alms; for an ascetic [*sannyasi*] who eagerly seeks alms attaches himself also to sensual enjoyments.

56. When no smoke ascends from the kitchen, when the pestle lies motionless, when the embers have been extinguished, when the people have finished their meal, when the remnants in the dishes have been removed, let the ascetic always go to beg.

57. Let him not be sorry when he obtains nothing, nor rejoice when he obtains something, let him accept so much only as will sustain life. . . .

59. By eating little, and by standing and sitting in solitude, let him restrain his senses, if they are attracted by sensual objects.

60. By the restraint of his senses, by the destruction of love and hatred, and by the abstention from injuring the creatures, he becomes fit for immortality.

85. A twice-born man who becomes an ascetic, after the successive performance of the above-mentioned acts, shakes off sin here below and reaches the highest Brahman.

86. Thus the law valid for self-restrained ascetics has been explained to you; now listen to the particular duties of those who give up the rites prescribed by the Veda:

87. The student, the householder, the hermit, and the ascetic, these constitute four separate orders, which all spring from the order of householders.

88. But all or even any of these orders, assumed successively in accordance with the Institutes of the sacred law, lead the Brahmana who acts by the preceding rules to the highest state.

89. And in accordance with the precepts of the Veda and of the Smriti, the housekeeper is declared to be superior to all of them; for he supports the other three.

90. As all rivers, both great and small, find a resting-place in the ocean, even so men of all orders find protection with householders.

91. By twice-born men belonging to any of these four orders, the tenfold law must be ever carefully obeyed.

92. Contentment, forgiveness, self-control, abstention from unrighteously appropriating anything, obedience to the roles of purification, coercion of the organs, wisdom, knowledge of the supreme Soul, truthfulness, and abstention from anger, form the tenfold law.

93. Those Brahmanas who thoroughly study the tenfold law, and after studying obey it, enter the highest state.[1]

[Book VI]

N O T E

1. From Georg Bühler, translator, *The Laws of Manu* (1969 edition). To improve readability, I have deleted the parentheses enclosing a number of emendations the translator has made to the original text.—Ed.

13. Ashtavakra Gita

"How can knowledge be acquired? How can liberation be attained?" These questions asked by King Janaka of the sage Ashtavakra begin the *Ashtavakra Gita* (also called the *Ashtavakra Samhita*). The remainder of this scripture on nondualistic Vedanta is a response to these questions. Ashtavakra tells Janaka that one must first develop the qualities of forgiveness, kindness, and other virtues, and then, while recognizing the world to be constantly passing away, meditate on the Atman within. The *Ashtavakra Gita,* therefore, accepts the basic thesis of nondualistic Vedanta: that the phenomenal world of experience is unreal, but that behind it lies the ultimate Reality which is its basis. In order to escape *samsara* (the cycle of birth and death), we must free ourselves from the desire for phenomenal things by discriminating between the Real and the unreal. Once we know the Atman to be our real Self and one with Brahman, the all-pervasive Reality, we are liberated.

In its complete form, the *Ashtavakra Gita* contains twenty-one chapters. King Janaka and Ashtavakra are both mentioned in the *Mahabharata,* and Janaka is again found in the *Brihadaranyaka Upanishad.* The date of composition of the *Ashtavakra Gita* is unknown.

The translator has provided a commentary, which we have included, in part.

Ashtavakra Gita

Janaka

1. How can knowledge be acquired? How can liberation be attained? How is renunciation possible? Tell me this, O Lord.

Knowledge is realization of the identity of the individual self and the Supreme Self or Brahman which is Existence-Knowledge-

Bliss Absolute [*Sat-chit-ananda*]. Liberation is freedom from ignorance, all bondage and limitations. . . .

Renunciation is unattachment to the pleasure and pain derived from worldly objects and even to the joyful life in heaven, which is also impermanent. . . . Unattachment is not indifference; nor is it the suppression of natural feelings of pleasure and pain. Attachment springs from the concept of duality, the idea that there are more entities than one. . . . The individual is Consciousness identified with his own body, mind, and senses. . . . As long as this identification persists, the individual's relationship with the world will be based upon this sense of difference.

Ashtavakra

2. If you aspire after liberation, my child, shun the objects of the senses as poison and seek forgiveness, sincerity, kindness, contentment, and truth as nectar.

7. You are the one seer of all and are really ever free. Verily, this alone is your bondage that you see yourself not as the seer but as something other.

One seer—The Self is the only subject, the entire universe being the object. *Bondage*—which consists in identifying the Self, which is the witness of the universe, with the body, mind, and the universe.

9. Burn down the forest of ignorance with the fire of the conviction that "I am the One" and "Pure Consciousness" and be free from grief and be happy.

10. You are that Consciousness, Bliss—Supreme Bliss, in and upon which this universe appears superimposed, like a snake upon a rope. Live happily.

Like a snake—This is an oft-repeated analogy of Advaita [nondualistic Vedanta]. In the dark of night a rope can be mistaken for a snake. The rope does not really become a snake; it has no other reality than the rope itself. . . . It is the Self—Pure Consciousness and Supreme Bliss—in which this universe, through ignorance, is seen to exist. . . . we must cease identifying ourselves with the superimposed universe, and thus we shall be happy.

11. He who considers himself free is free indeed, and he who considers himself bound remains bound. "As one thinks, so one becomes" is a popular saying in the world, and it is quite true.

In reality the Self is ever free; it never enters into a state of bondage. It is [through] our ignorance we think ourselves bound, and this thought makes our supposed bondage persist. . . . If, however, we constantly think of ourselves as the eternally free Self, we shall realize that we are ever free.

[Chap. I]

Janaka

1. Oh, I am spotless, tranquil, Pure Consciousness, and beyond nature. All this time I have been merely duped by illusion.

Having attained spiritual illumination through the instruction of Ashtavakra, Janaka now expresses the joy of Self-realization in the following verses:

4. As waves, foam, and bubbles are not different from water, so the universe emanating from the Self is not different from it.

The Atman is the only substance of the universe, just as clay is the only substance of a pot. The pot is nothing but clay with name and form superimposed on it. So is this universe nothing but the Self with name and form superimposed on it.

7. The world appears from the ignorance of the Self and disappears with the knowledge of Self, just as the snake appears from noncognition of the rope and disappears with its recognition.

An illusion persists only so long as we do not recognize the object on which the illusion has been superimposed. When we know the rope to be a rope, the snake-knowledge vanishes. Similarly, the world does not really exist, yet through ignorance it appears to exist, and it disappears with the knowledge of the Self on which the illusion of the world is superimposed.

16. Oh, the root of misery is duality! There is no other remedy for it except the realization that all objects of experience are unreal and that I am pure, One, Consciousness, and Bliss.

[Chap. II]

Ashtavakra

1. Having known yourself as really indestructible and One, how is it that you, knower of the Self and serene, feel attached to the acquisition of wealth?

The dialogue between Ashtavakra and Janaka brings out very clearly the exact condition and status of one who is firmly established in Self-knowledge. The difference between an ignorant man and one of Self-knowledge lies not in the actions they perform, but in the consciousness with which they perform them. In the case of the man of Self-knowledge, such consciousness is not easily perceived by ordinary people. Therefore, although the two people outwardly appear to be the same, they are actually poles apart.

4. After hearing oneself to be Pure Consciousness and surpassingly beautiful, how can one yet be deeply attached to sensual objects and thus become impure?

Self-knowledge and the lust for sensual objects cannot exist together. He who has known the Self cannot find anything else beautiful and attractive, and cannot become attached to anything.

14. He who has given up worldly attachment . . . who is beyond the pairs of opposites, and who is free from desire—to him no experience, as a matter of course, can cause either pleasure or pain.

All our pleasures and pains arise from the contact of the senses with pleasure-giving or pain-producing objects, thus causing us to desire the former and hate the latter. But if we feel neither attraction nor repulsion for sense objects, and allow them to come as a matter of course, they cannot produce any pleasurable or painful sensations. . . .

[Chap. III]

2. The Universe rises from you like bubbles rising from the sea. Thus know the Self to be One and in this way enter into the state of dissolution.

3. The Universe, because it is unreal, being manifested like the

snake in the rope, does not exist in you who are pure, even though it is present to the senses. Therefore in this way enter into the state of dissolution.

[Chap. V]

Janaka

2. I am like the ocean and the universe is like the wave; this is knowledge. So it has neither to be renounced nor accepted nor destroyed.

Water is the real substance [in this example]; the name and form of the wave are only apparent. Similarly, the Self is the only substance; the name and form of the universe are only illusory superimpositions.

[Chap. VII]

Ashtavakra

1. It is bondage when the mind desires or grieves at anything, rejects or accepts anything, feels happy or angry at anything.

2. Liberation is attained when the mind does not desire or grieve or reject or accept or feel happy or angry.

4. When there is no I, there is liberation; when there is I, there is bondage. Considering this, refrain from accepting or rejecting anything.

[Chap. VIII]

2. Rare indeed, my child, is that blessed person whose desire for life, enjoyment, and learning has been extinguished by observing the ways of men.

Some people learn the hollowness of the world by observation. By observing the suffering of others they realize that the world cannot give eternal happiness.

8. Desires alone are the world. Do you, therefore, renounce them all. The renunciation of desire is the renunciation of the world. Now you may live anywhere.

[Chap. IX]

2. Look upon friends, lands, wealth, houses, wives, presents, and other such marks of good fortune as a dream or juggler's show, lasting only a few days.

[Chap. X]

3. He who has known for certain that adversity and prosperity come in their own good time through the effects of past actions is ever contented, has all the senses under control, and neither desires nor grieves.

[Chap. XI]

Janaka

4. Having nothing to accept and nothing to reject, and having neither joy nor sorrow, thus, sir, do I now firmly abide.

[Chap. XII]

3. Fully realizing that nothing whatsoever is really done by the Self, I do whatever presents itself to be done and so I live happily.

[Chap. XIII]

2. When desire has melted away, where then are my riches, where my friends, where are the robbers in the form of sense objects, where the scriptures, and where knowledge?

The objects of sense rob us of the perception of the Self. Scriptural injunctions are only for those who are in ignorance. They are of no use to a man of Self-realization.

[Chap. XIV]

Ashtavakra

1. A man of pure intellect realizes the Self even by instruction casually imparted. A man of impure intellect is bewildered in trying to realize the Self even after enquiring throughout life.

"Pure" indicates that the intellect has been freed from the elements of *rajas* [passion] and *tamas* [darkness], and is full of *sattva* [light].

2. Nonattachment for sense objects is liberation; love for sense

objects is bondage. Such, verily is Knowledge. Now do as you please.

[Chap. XV]

11. The liberated one is always found abiding in the Self and is pure in heart; he lives freed from all desires, under all conditions.

[Chap. XVII]

59. With perfect equanimity, even in practical life, the wise one sits happily, sleeps happily, moves happily, speaks happily, and eats happily.

65. Blessed indeed is that knower of the Self who has transcended the mind, and who, even though seeing, hearing, touching, smelling, or eating, is the same under all conditions.

[Chap. XVIII]

Janaka

3. Where is the past, where is the future, where, even, is the present? Where is space, and where, even, is eternity for me who abide in my own glory?[1]

[Chap. XIX]

NOTE

1. From Swami Nityaswarupananda, translator and commentator, *Ashtav-akra Samhita* (1969).

14. Shankara

Philosopher, prophet, reformer—Shankara was all of these. As the brilliant propounder of nondualistic Vedanta, his commentaries, philosophical works, and monastic ideals still guide and shape Indian religion. Although his contributions to Vedantic thought are well known, the facts concerning his personal history remain relatively obscure. Shankara was born in A.D. 686 of Brahmin parents at Kaladi, a small village of western Malabar, in southern India. By the age of ten he was an intellectual prodigy, having read and memorized all the significant scriptures and written commentaries on a number of them. But even at this tender age, Shankara had tired of intellectual feats and had begun to realize the emptiness of mere book-knowledge. It was at this time he wrote his immortal poem, "The Shattering of Illusion," which clearly expressed a suspicion of worldly happiness and served as a prelude to his renunciation of the world as a monk. It also demonstrates his remarkable power of discrimination, which was to characterize all his writings in the years to follow.

Shankara's life came to an end at the age of thirty-two. But during these few years he had established ten monastic orders, founded four well-known monasteries, and produced a prodigious amount of philosophical literature: commentaries on the *Vedanta Sutras,* the principal Upanishads, and the *Bhagavad-Gita;* as well as major philosophical works, among them the *Upadeshasahasri* and the *Viveka-Chudamani (Crest-Jewel of Discrimination).* He was also author of many poems, hymns, prayers, and minor works on Vedanta.

Fundamentally, Shankara's philosophy may be summed up by this statement from one of his works: "Brahman—the absolute existence, knowledge, and bliss—is real. The universe is not real. Brahman and Atman are one." That which is real never changes;

it is ever the same. This changeless Reality is pure consciousness, the constant feature of all our experiences; for it is the basis of our three states of ordinary consciousness—waking, dreaming, and dreamless sleep. This world of changing phenomena Shankara calls *maya,* which appears real to those in ignorance, but illusory or totally insubstantial to the illumined soul. The purpose of life is to transcend maya and discover the bliss of the Atman, which is one with Brahman.

The *Viveka-Chudamani* is written in the form of a dialogue between teacher and disciple. Basically, it establishes the prerequisities for following the yoga of knowledge *(jnana yoga),* as well as describing the methods of discrimination between the Real and the unreal by which spiritual wisdom can be attained. *A Garland of Questions and Answers (Prasnottara Malika),* a part of which follows, is one of Shankara's minor works, in his popular dialogue style.

Shankara

From *Viveka-Chudamani*

Only through God's grace may we obtain those three rarest advantages—human birth, the longing for liberation, and discipleship to an illumined teacher.

Nevertheless, there are those who somehow manage to obtain this rare human birth, together with bodily and mental strength, and an understanding of the scriptures—and yet are so deluded that they do not struggle for liberation. Such men are suicides. They clutch at the unreal and destroy themselves.

For what greater fool can there be than the man who has obtained this rare human birth together with bodily and mental strength and yet fails, through delusion, to realize his own highest good?

Men may recite the scriptures and sacrifice to the holy spirits, they may perform rituals and worship deities—but, until a man wakes to knowledge of his identity with the Atman, liberation can never be obtained; no, not even at the end of many hundreds of ages.

The scriptures declare that immortality cannot be gained through work or progeny or riches, but by renunciation alone. Hence it is clear that work cannot bring us liberation.

Therefore, let the wise man give up craving for pleasure in external things, and struggle hard for liberation. Let him seek out a noble and high-souled teacher, and become absorbed whole-heartedly in the truth which is taught him.

Through devotion to right discrimination he will climb to the height of union with Brahman. By the power of the Atman, let him rescue his own soul which lies drowned in the vast waters of worldliness.

Let the wise, who have grown tranquil and who practice contemplation of the Atman, give up all worldly activities and struggle to cut the bonds of worldliness.

Right action helps to purify the heart, but it does not give us direct perception of the Reality. The Reality is attained through discrimination, but not in the smallest degree by ten million acts.

Correct discernment shows us the true nature of a rope, and removes the painful fear caused by our deluded belief that it is a large snake.

Certain knowledge of the Reality is gained only through meditation upon right teaching, and not by sacred ablutions, or alms-giving, or by the practice of hundreds of breathing exercises.

[Verses 3-13]

A man should be intelligent and learned, with great powers of comprehension, and able to overcome doubts by the exercise of his reason. One who has these qualifications is fitted for knowledge of the Atman.

He alone may be considered qualified to seek Brahman who has discrimination, whose mind is turned away from all enjoyments, who possesses tranquillity and the kindred virtues, and who feels a longing for liberation.

In this connection, the sages have spoken of four qualifications for attainment. When these are present, devotion to the Reality will become complete. When they are absent, it will fail.

First is mentioned discrimination between the eternal and the non-eternal. Next comes renunciation of the enjoyment of the fruits of action, here and hereafter. Then come the six treasures of virtue, beginning with tranquillity. And last, certainly, is the longing for liberation.

Brahman is real; the universe is unreal. A firm conviction that this is so is called *discrimination* between the eternal and the non-eternal.

Renunciation is the giving-up of all the pleasures of the eyes, the ears, and the other senses, the giving-up of all objects of transitory enjoyment, the giving-up of the desire for a physical body as well as for the highest kind of spirit-body of a god.

To detach the mind from all objective things by continually seeing their imperfection, and to direct it steadfastly toward Brahman, its goal—this is called *tranquillity*.

To detach both kinds of sense-organs—those of perception and those of action—from objective things, and to withdraw them to rest in their respective centers—this is called *self-control*. True *mental poise* consists in not letting the mind react to external stimuli.

To endure all kinds of afflictions without rebellion, complaint or lament—this is called *forbearance*.

A firm convicton, based upon intellectual understanding, that the teachings of the scriptures and of one's master are true—this is called by the sages the *faith* which leads to realization of the Reality.

To concentrate the intellect repeatedly upon the pure Brahman and to keep it fixed there always—this is called *self-surrender*. This does not mean soothing the mind, like a baby, with idle thoughts.

Longing for liberation is the will to be free from the fetters forged by ignorance—beginning with the ego-sense and so on, down to the physical body itself—through the realization of one's true nature.

Even though this longing for liberation may be present in a slight or moderate degree, it will grow intense through the grace of the teacher, and through the practice of renunciation and of virtues such as tranquillity, etc. And it will bear fruit.

When renunciation and the longing for liberation are present to an intense degree within a man, then the practice of tranquillity and the other virtues will bear fruit and lead to the goal.

Where renunciation and longing for liberation are weak, tranquillity and the other virtues are a mere appearance, like the mirage in the desert.

Among all means of liberation, devotion is supreme. To seek earnestly to know one's real nature—this is said to be *devotion*.

In other words, devotion can be defined as the search for the reality of one's own Atman. The seeker after the reality of the Atman, who possesses the above-mentioned qualifications, should approach an illumined teacher from whom he can learn the way to liberation from all bondage.

[16-32]

Faith, devotion, and constant union with God through prayer—these are declared by the sacred scriptures to be the seeker's direct means of liberation. To him who abides by them comes liberation from that bondage of physical consciousness which has been forged by ignorance.

Because you are associated with ignorance, the supreme Atman within you appears to be in bondage to the non-Atman. This is the sole cause of the cycle of births and deaths. The flame of illumination, which is kindled by discrimination between Atman and non-Atman, will burn away the effects of ignorance, down to their very roots.

The Disciple speaks:

Master, please listen to the questions I am about to ask. I shall feel blessed if I may hear an answer from your lips.

What, in reality, is this bondage? How did it begin? In what is it rooted? How is a man set free from it? What is the non-Atman? What is the supreme Atman? How can one discriminate between them? Please answer me.

The Master speaks:

You are blessed indeed! You are drawing near to the goal. Through you, your whole family have become purified, because you long to get free from the bondage of ignorance and reach Brahman.

Children may free their father from his debts, but no other person can free a man from his bondage: he must do it himself.

Others may relieve the suffering caused by a burden that weighs upon the head; but the suffering which comes from hunger and the like can only be relieved by one's self.

The sick man who takes medicine and follows the rules of diet is seen to be restored to health—but not through the efforts of another.

A clear vision of the Reality may be obtained only through our own eyes, when they have been opened by spiritual insight—never through the eyes of some other seer. Through our own eyes we learn what the moon looks like: how could we learn this through the eyes of others?

Those cords that bind us, because of our ignorance, our lustful desires and the fruits of our karma—how could anybody but ourselves untie them, even in the course of innumerable ages?

Neither by the practice of Yoga or of Sankhya philosophy, nor by good works, nor by learning, does liberation come; but only through a realization that Atman and Brahman are one—in no other way.

It is the duty of a king to please his people, but not everybody who pleases the people is fit to be a king. For the people can be pleased by the beauty of a *vina*'s form, and the skill with which its strings are plucked.

Erudition, well-articulated speech, a wealth of words, and skill in expounding the scriptures—these things give pleasure to the learned, but they do not bring liberation.

Study of the scriptures is fruitless as long as Brahman has not been experienced. And when Brahman has been experienced, it is useless to read the scriptures.

A network of words is like a dense forest which causes the mind to wander hither and thither. Therefore, those who know this truth should struggle hard to experience Brahman.

When a man has been bitten by the snake of ignorance he can only be cured by the realization of Brahman. What use are Vedas or scriptures, charms or herbs?

A sickness is not cured by saying the word "medicine." You must take the medicine. Liberation does not come by merely saying the word "Brahman." Brahman must be actually experienced.

Until you allow this apparent universe to dissolve from your consciousness—until you have experienced Brahman—how can you find liberation just by saying the word "Brahman"? The result is merely a noise.

Until a man has destroyed his enemies and taken possession of the splendour and wealth of the kingdom, he cannot become a king by simply saying: "I am a king."

A buried treasure is not uncovered by merely uttering the words "come forth." You must follow the right directions, dig, remove the stones and earth from above it, and then make it your own. In the same way, the pure truth of the Atman, which is buried under Maya and the effects of Maya, can be reached by meditation, contemplation and other spiritual disciplines such as a knower of Brahman may prescribe—but never by subtle arguments.

Therefore the wise must personally exert all their powers to get liberation from the bondage of the world, just as they would personally take remedies against physical ailments.

[46-66]

The spiritual seeker who is possessed of tranquillity, self-control, mental poise and forbearance, devotes himself to the practice of contemplation, and meditates upon the Atman within himself as the Atman within all beings. Thus he completely destroys the sense of separateness which arises from the darkness of ignorance, and dwells in joy, identifying himself with Brahman, free from distracting thoughts and selfish occupations.

[355]

Be devoted to Brahman and you will be able to control your senses. Control your senses and you will gain mastery over your mind. Master your mind, and the sense of ego will be dissolved. In this manner, the yogi achieves an unbroken realization of the joy of Brahman. Therefore let the seeker strive to give his heart to Brahman.

[368]

Only the man who has intense dispassion can attain samadhi. He who has attained samadhi lives in a state of constant illumination. The illumined heart is liberated from bondage. The liberated man alone experiences eternal joy.

[375]

Our perception of the universe is a continuous perception of Brahman, though the ignorant man is not aware of this. Indeed, this universe is nothing but Brahman. See Brahman everywhere, under all circumstances, with the eye of the spirit and a tranquil heart. How can the physical eyes see anything but physical objects? How can the mind of the enlightened man think of anything other than the Reality?

How could a wise man reject the experience of supreme bliss and take delight in mere outward forms? When the moon shines in its exceeding beauty, who would care to look at a painted moon?

Experience of the unreal offers us no satisfaction, nor any escape from misery. Find satisfaction, therefore, in the experience of the sweet bliss of Brahman. Devote yourself to the Atman and live happily forever.

O noble soul, this is how you must pass your days—see the Atman everywhere, enjoy the bliss of the Atman, fix your thought upon the Atman, the one without a second.

The Atman is one, absolute, indivisible. It is pure consciousness. To imagine many forms within it is like imagining palaces in the air. Therefore, know that you are the Atman, ever-blissful, one without a second, and find the ultimate peace. Remain absorbed in the joy which is silence.

This state of silence is a state of entire peace, in which the intellect ceases to occupy itself with the unreal. In this silence, the great soul who knows and is one with Brahman enjoys unmingled bliss forever.[1]

[521-526]

The Shattering of Illusion

(Moha Mudgaram)
Who is thy wife? Who is thy son?
The ways of this world are strange indeed.

Whose art thou? Whence art thou come?
Vast is thy ignorance, my beloved.
Therefore ponder these things and worship the Lord.

Behold the folly of Man:
In childhood busy with his toys,
In youth bewitched by love,
In age bowed down with cares—
And always unmindful of the Lord!
The hours fly, the seasons roll, life ebbs,
But the breeze of hope blows continually in his heart.

Birth brings death, death brings rebirth:
This evil needs no proof.
Where then, O Man, is thy happiness?
This life trembles in the balance
Like water on a lotus-leaf—
And yet the sage can show us, in an instant,
How to bridge this sea of change.

When the body is wrinkled, when the hair turns grey,
When the gums are toothless, and the old man's staff
Shakes like a reed beneath his weight,
The cup of his desire is still full.

Thy son may bring thee suffering,
Thy wealth is no assurance of heaven:
Therefore be not vain of thy wealth,
Or of thy family, or of thy youth—
All are fleeting, all must change.
Know this and be free.
Enter the joy of the Lord.

Seek neither peace nor strife
With kith or kin, with friend or foe.
O beloved, if thou wouldst attain freeedom,
Be equal unto all.

A Garland of Questions and Answers

(*Prasnottara Malika*)

What is the best thing a spiritual aspirant can do? Carry out his guru's instructions.

What must be avoided? Deeds which lead us into greater ignorance of the truth.

Who is a guru? He who has found the truth of Brahman and is always concerned for the welfare of his disciples.

What is the first and most important duty for a man of right understanding? To cut through the bonds of worldly desire.

How can one be liberated? By attaining the knowledge of Brahman.

Who, in this world, can be called pure? He whose mind is pure.

Who can be called wise? He who can discriminate between the real and the unreal.

What deludes a man like an intoxicating drink? Attachment to the objects of the senses.

What causes the bondage of worldly desire? Thirst to enjoy those objects.

What is the obstacle to spiritual growth? Laziness.

In this world, what is the greatest terror? The fear of death.

Who is awake? He who practices discrimination.

Who is asleep? He who lives in ignorance.

What roll quickly away, like drops of water from a lotus leaf? Youth, wealth and the years of a man's life.

What is happiness? Detachment.

What are worthless as soon as they are won? Honor and fame.

What brings happiness? The friendship of the holy.

What is death? Ignorance.

What should a man think of, day and night? He should think how transitory this world is. He should never think thoughts of lust.

Who avoids the snares of this world? He who is truthful and who is able to remain unmoved by either pleasure or pain and all life's other pairs of opposites.

To whom do the gods themselves pay homage? To him who is compassionate.

Whom do all men respect? Him who is humble and speaks the truth so that it does good to others and makes them happy.

What is a man's best ornament? His good character.

What qualities are rarest in this world? To have the gift of speaking sweet words with compassion, to be learned without pride, to be heroic and also forgiving, to be rich without attachment to riches—these four are rare.

Who is revered by the wise? He who is humble.

What are the enemies of a spiritual aspirant? Lust and greed.

Wherein lies strength? In patience.

What is fearlessness? Dispassion.

What is most rarely found among mankind? Love for the Lord.

Who is dear to the Lord? He who is fearless and takes away fear from others.

How does one attain liberation? By practicing spiritual disciplines.

Who are our enemies? Our sense-organs, when they are uncontrolled.

Who are our friends? Our sense-organs, when they are controlled.

Who has overcome the world? He who has conquered his own mind.

What are the duties of a spiritual aspirant? To keep company with the holy, to renounce all thoughts of "me" and "mine," to devote himself to God.[2]

NOTES

1. This selection and the one following from Swami Prabhavananda and Christopher Isherwood, translators, *Shankara's Crest-Jewel of Discrimination* (*Viveka-Chudamani*) (1947).

2. Ibid. (1970, paperback).

I V

THE MYSTIC–POETS

15. Tiruvalluvar

The *Tirukkural*, a long poem written in Tamil by the poet Tiruvalluvar, has been called the fifth Veda as well as the Tamil Bible of south India. In fact, when reading the *Tirukkural* one is struck by its great similarity in thought and expression to the Christian Bible. Various dates have been assigned to the poem's composition; the most reliable seems to be the first century A.D.

The length of the *Tirukkural* runs to 1,330 verses.

Very little is known about the author. Even his real name is a mystery, for Tiruvalluvar simply means "a *Valluva* (or pariah) devotee." It is known, however, that he worked as a weaver in Mylapore, Madras, and lived an exceedingly happy family life until the death of his wife, Vasuki, who was a model of every wifely virtue. It is said that Tiruvalluvar then renounced the world to become an ascetic.

Tiruvalluvar

From the *Tirukkural*

24. Behold the man whose firm will controlleth his five senses even as the goading hook controlleth the elephant: he is a seed fit for the fields of heaven.

34. Be pure in heart: all righteousness is contained in this one commandment: all other things are nought but empty display.

72. Those that love not live only for themselves: as to those that love, they will give their very bones for helping others.

80. The seat of life is in Love: the man who hath it not is only a mass of skin-encased bone.

128. If even one word of thine causeth pain to another, all thy virtue is lost.

162. No blessing is so great as a nature that is free from all envy.

207. There is a way of escape from every other enemy: but ill deeds never die but pursue and destroy their author.

211. The gracious expect no return when they oblige: how can the world ever repay the rain-cloud?

261. Patient endurance of suffering and non-injuring of life, in these is contained the whole of *tapas*.

274. Behold the man who taketh cover under a saintly garb and doth evil: he is like a fowler hiding in the bush and decoying birds.

336. But yesterday a man was and to-day he is not: that is the wonder of wonders in this world.

346. The feelings of *I* and *Mine* are nought but vanity and pride: he who crusheth them entereth a higher world than the world of the Gods.

350. Attach and tie thyself to Him who hath conquered all attachments: bind thyself firmly to Him in order that all thy bonds may be broken.

354. Though risen to human birth, the soul hath profited nothing if it hath not realized the Truth.

441. Esteem thou the men that have grown old in righteousness, and acquire their friendship.

597. Men of spirit lose not their heart when they meet with defeat: the elephant planteth his legs only more firmly when he is hit by the deep-piercing arrow.

679. Placate and make friends with thy enemies even more swiftly than thou rewardest friends.

787. That man alone is thy friend who turneth thee aside from wrong, directeth thee toward the right, and beareth thee company in misfortune.

985. It is humility that is the strength of the strong: and that is also the armor of the man of worth against his foes.[1]

NOTE

1. From V. V. S. Aiyar, translator, *The Kural or the Maxims of Tiruvalluvar* (1952).

16. Bhartrihari

The *Vairagya-Satakam* or *Hundred Verses on Renunciation* by Bhartrihari is a remarkable collection of terse, and often pungent, verses that reflect the inner struggles, doubts, and joys of a spiritual aspirant. Bhartrihari, however, was no ordinary aspirant. According to tradition, he was King of Ujjaini in central India. Bhartrihari wearied of a life of pleasure and most likely in middle age renounced his kingdom and retreated to an isolated region to practice austerities. In time, he became a great yogi and an illumined soul.

Bhartrihari was the author of three well-known works: *Nitisatakam (Hundred Verses on Worldly Wisdom); Sringara-Satakam (Hundred Verses on Love);* and *Vairagya Satakam (Hundred Verses on Renunciation).*

Bhartrihari

Verses on Renunciation

1

All glory to Shiva!
Light of Knowledge!
Who dwells in the shrine of the yogis' hearts
Who dispels the gloom of ignorance that overcasts our minds
And in whose wake all goodness and prosperity follow;
O Shiva, destroyer of lust,
How your face shines—like the fresh bloom of budding flowers!

7

Nay, I have been no consumer of worldly pleasures;
It is they, rather, which have consumed me.

No penances have burned away my sins;
It is my sins that have scorched my heart.
Time will not pass away;
'Tis we who pass away in death.
Though now I grow old and feeble
Desire, alas, does not grow feeble.

8

Wrinkles crease my careworn face,
Withered are my limbs,
And snowy white my hair.
Craving alone retains its youth.

18

Through ignorance
The moth becomes
A sacrifice to fire,
And the fish to the baited hook;
Yet we, though blessed with intellect,
Still yield to fleshly cravings.
Alas, how inscrutable is this world's delusion!

31

With enjoyment
Comes fear of disease;
With social position,
Fear of disfavor;
With riches,
Fear of hostile kings;
With honor,
Fear of humiliation;
With power,
Fear of an enemy;
With beauty,
Fear of old age;
With scholarship,
Fear of challengers;
With virtue,

Fear of traducers;
With the body,
Fear of death.
Everything in this world is fraught with fear;
Renunciation alone makes one fearless.

32

Birth is ever threatened by death,
Youth by old age,
Contentment by avarice,
The joy of a disciplined mind by wanton women,
Virtuous behavior by jealous men,
Forest walks by beasts of prey,
Kings by corrupt ministers;
The greatest powers, even, must yield at last to time.
Indeed, what is there in this world without an enemy?

34

Like waves which tremble at their crest,
Are life's enjoyments;
And as speedily does life itself dissolve.
The joys of love bear us afloat
For but a few days,
Only to sink at last.
O teachers of mankind!
You, who have realized the ephemeral nature of this world,
You, whose hearts melt with compassion,
Lead men across
This ocean of worldliness.

35

Like the play of lightning
Among the clouds,
Are the fleeting enjoyments of life;
Capricious, indeed, are the cravings of youth.
Life trembles
Like a drop of water
On the edge of a lotus leaf.

Then lo! it is swallowed by the wind!
The wise fix their mind in Truth,
Which comes to all who live
In the calm of self-surrender.

38

Like a tigress
Old age waits for us,
And we grow afraid;
Like the army of the foe
Disease assaults the body;
Life drains from us
Like water from a leaking cup.
Yet, how very strange it is,
Still man abandons not his foolish ways.

40

There is one joy
And one only
That is lasting, unchanging, supreme;
Which, once tasted, makes tasteless
The glory and enjoyment derived from the sovereignty
    of the three worlds;*
And makes the powers and pleasures of the gods
    seem like straw.
O Sadhu
Yearn for no other joy but that.

62

O my mind
Why dost thou wander
In such vain pursuits?
Remain poised.
Whatever happens
Happens of itself
Not otherwise;

* The "three worlds" are the sky, the earth, and the nether world.

Thinking not of past or future
Let me wait serene for what may come.

68

When there is longing for liberation,
And devotion to Lord Shiva;
When there is no attachment to family
And passion's lusting;
When there is the silence
Of the forest
Unbroken by human voice,
And renunciation rules our lives;
What higher bliss can be wished for?

69

What can one gain
From all this worry over things
Essentially unreal?
Meditate alone on the supreme Brahman,
Infinite, ageless, and effulgent,
In whose light
The fleeting enjoyments of the world
Seem pitiable, indeed.

85

Seated peacefully alone
When all sounds are hushed into silence
And the banks of the river shimmer
Beneath the moon's soft glow
A fear of future birth and death
Invades my heart;
Aloud I cry:
"Shiva! Shiva! Shiva!"
Ah, when shall my eyes shed tears of ecstasy?

94

Earth is his bed,
His arms a pillow,

The sky his canopy;
The genial breeze a fan,
His lamp the autumn moon,
And dispassion his wife.
Thus the sage rejoices,
And like some noble monarch
Reclines at ease, and in peace.

100

O mother earth!
O wind, my father!
O fire, my friend!
O water, my kinsman!
O sky my noble brother!
I salute you all.
Through merits
Won by thy assistance
Pure knowledge now is mine,
And blind infatuation's power is crushed.
O Brahman, now I merge at last with thee![1]

N O T E

1. From Bhartrihari, *Vairagya Satakam* (selections translated by Swami Prabhavananda and Clive Johnson).

17. Kabir

The mystic-poet Kabir (1440-1518) is a delightful and fascinating blend of two major faiths—Hinduism and Islam—and an honor to both of them. His poetry, which bursts upon the reader like a fresh breeze from the sea, is the song of his soul. He opens his heart, and we gaze at the richness within. Kabir was most probably born in Benares of Mohammedan parents, but early in life became a disciple of the famous Hindu ascetic Ramananda. He approached Ramananda for initiation on numerous occasions, but was met with refusal each time. At length, in order to obtain his desire, Kabir one morning hid upon the steps leading to the river Ganges, where Ramananda was accustomed to bathe. The result was that his master stepped on him by surprise, and uttered, "Ram! Ram!", the name of his chosen deity. Kabir at once considered himself initiated, and it appears that Ramananda accepted him—though perhaps with a smile.

Unlike many of the traditional holy men of the Orient, Kabir never undertook ascetic practices or retired from the world. He was married, a father of children, and a weaver by trade. He found it impossible to accept any path that led away from a world he saw filled only with beauty and joy. To Kabir, God has "spread His form of love throughout *all* the world." In an orthodox atmosphere such as Benares, Kabir was looked upon as a heretic. Pressures against him became so great that in 1495 he was ordered by the ruling king to leave. The remainder of his life was spent in various cities of northern India, singing his songs, and spreading his gospel of divine love. At last, in 1518, broken in health and with hands too feeble to play the music he loved, he passed away.

Kabir

O servant, where dost thou seek Me?
Lo! I am beside thee.
I am neither in temple nor in mosque:
    I am neither in Kaaba nor in Kailash*
Neither am I in rites and ceremonies,
    nor in Yoga and renunciation.
If thou art a true seeker, thou shalt at
    once see Me: thou shalt meet Me in a moment
    of time.
Kabir says, "O Sadhu! God is the breath of all
    breath."

ॐ

Within this earthen vessel are bowers and groves,
    and within it is the Creator:
Within this vessel are the seven oceans and the
    unnumbered stars.
The touchstone and the jewel-appraiser are within;
And within this vessel the Eternal soundeth, and the
    spring wells up.
Kabir says: "Listen to me, my friend! My beloved
    Lord is within."

ॐ

My body and my mind are grieved for the want of Thee;
O my Beloved, come to my house!
When people say I am Thy bride, I am ashamed;
    for I have not touched Thy heart with my heart.
Then what is this love of mine? I have no taste
    for food, I have no sleep; my heart is ever
    restless within doors and without.

---

   * Places sacred to worshipers of Mohammed and Shiva, at once indicating Kabir's lifelong refusal to align himself with any particular creed or religion.

As water is to the thirsty, so is the lover to the
   bride. Who is there that will carry my news to
   my beloved?
Kabir is restless: he is dying for sight of Him.

৯৯

The lock of error shuts the gate, open it with the
   key of love:
Thus, by opening the door, thou shalt wake the Beloved.
Kabir says: "O brother! do not pass by such good
   fortune as this."

৯৯

I have stilled my restless mind, and my heart
   is radiant: for in Thatness I have seen beyond
   Thatness, in company I have seen the Comrade
   Himself.
Living in bondage, I have set myself free: I have
   broken away from the clutch of all narrowness.
Kabir says: "I have attained the unattainable, and
   my heart is coloured with the colour of love."

৯৯

O Man, if thou dost not know thine own Lord, whereof
   art thou so proud?
Put thy cleverness away: mere words shall never
   unite thee to Him.
Do not deceive thyself with the witness of the
   Scriptures:
Love is something other than this, and he who has
   sought it truly has found it.

৯৯

Between the poles of the conscious and the unconscious,
   there has the mind made a swing:
Thereon hang all beings and all worlds, and that
   swing never ceases its sway.
Millions of beings are there: the sun and the
   moon in their courses are there:

Millions of ages pass, and the swing goes on.
All swing! the sky and the earth and the air and
the water; and the Lord Himself taking form:
And the sight of this has made Kabir a servant.

ह

O Sadhu! the simple union is the best.
Since the day when I met with my Lord, there has been
no end to the sport of our love.
I shut not my eyes, I close not my ears, I do not
mortify my body;
I see with eyes open and smile, and behold His
beauty everywhere:
I utter His Name, and whatever I see, it reminds
me of Him; whatever I do, it becomes His worship.
The rising and the setting are one to me; all con-
tradictions are solved.
Wherever I go, I move round Him,
All I achieve is His service:
When I lie down, I lie prostrate at His feet.
He is the only adorable one to me: I have none other.
My tongue has left off impure words, it sings His
glory day and night:
Whether I rise or sit down, I can never forget Him;
for the rhythm of His music beats in my ears.
Kabir says: "My heart is frenzied, and I disclose
in my soul what is hidden. I am immersed in that
one great bliss which transcends all pleasure and
pain."[1]

ह

NOTE

1. From Rabindranath Tagore, translator, with the assistance of Evelyn
Underhill, *One Hundred Poems of Kabir* (1954, Indian edition).

18. Sri Chaitanya

Sri Chaitanya (1485-1533), like many great saints before and after him, served as a vitalizing force in the Hindu religion. His philosophy of divine love has found its way into numerous hymns of Bengal, and his teachings greatly helped to usher in a renewed spirit of devotion in that part of India. Chaitanya was both a scholar and a lover of God. He founded a school of Sanskrit grammar and logic when only sixteen. At twenty-three, he experienced an ecstatic vision of Krishna while worshiping at Gaya (where Buddha also attained his illumination), and with this experience the scholar was transformed into a God-intoxicated devotee. At the age of twenty-five, Chaitanya renounced the world, leaving his home village of Navadvip, friends, and family. The story of his departure is one of the most popular subjects of Bengali drama and poetry.

During the final twelve years of his life, Chaitanya was almost constantly absorbed in communion with God (*samadhi*), and his overwhelming love for Krishna infected thousands, transforming their lives. He spent his final days in the holy city of Puri. It is said that he entered a temple near there and never came out again. The belief exists that in the image of that temple the spirit of Chaitanya lives on for eternity.

Sri Chaitanya

A Prayer

Chant the name of the Lord and His glory unceasingly
That the mirror of the heart may be wiped clean

And quenched that mighty forest fire,
Worldly lust, raging furiously within.

O Name, stream down in moonlight on the lotus-heart,
Opening its cup to knowledge of Thyself.
O self, drown deep in the waves of His bliss,
Chanting His Name continually,
Tasting His nectar at every step,
Bathing in His Name, that bath for weary souls.

Various are Thy Names, O Lord,
In each and every Name Thy power resides.
No times are set, no rites are needful, for chanting of
    Thy Name,
So vast is Thy mercy.
How huge, then, is my wretchedness
Who find, in this empty life and heart,
No devotion to Thy Name!

O my mind,
Be humbler than a blade of grass,
Be patient and forbearing like the tree,
Take no honour to thyself,
Give honour to all,
Chant unceasingly the Name of the Lord.

O Lord and Soul of the Universe,
Mine is no prayer for wealth or retinue,
The playthings of lust or the toys of fame;
As many times as I may be reborn
Grant me, O Lord, a steadfast love for Thee.

A drowning man in this world's fearful ocean
Is Thy servant, O Sweet One.
In Thy mercy
Consider him as dust beneath Thy feet.

Ah, how I long for the day
When, in chanting Thy Name, the tears will spill down
From my eyes, and my throat will refuse to utter

Its prayers, choking and stammering with ecstasy,
When all the hairs of my body will stand erect with joy!

Ah, how I long for the day
When an instant's separation from Thee, O Govinda,*
Will be as a thousand years,
When my heart burns away with its desire
And the world, without Thee, is a heartless void.

Prostrate at Thy feet let me be, in unwavering devotion,
Neither imploring the embrace of Thine arms
Nor bewailing the withdrawal of Thy Presence
Though it tears my soul asunder.
O Thou, who stealest the hearts of Thy devotees,
Do with me what Thou wilt—
For Thou art my heart's Beloved, Thou and Thou alone.[1]

NOTE

1. Translated by Swami Prabhavananda and Christopher Isherwood, in Christopher Isherwood, editor, *Vedanta for the Western World* (1961).

* Another name of Sri Krishna.

19. Mira Bai

Mira Bai (1547-1614) was one of the great woman poets of northern India whose ecstatic songs of love for Sri Krishna are still sung today throughout the country. At the age of eight she was betrothed to the son of the ruler of Mewar State, and at eighteen went to live with her husband, the young Raja Bojaraja, at the capital city of Chitor. Mira Bai was devoted to God from her early childhood, and she gathered many devotees about her at the palace. Difficulties began, however, when her young husband died and her brother-in-law assumed the throne. Certain relatives proved hostile to her beliefs, and even attempted to poison her. Eventually, Mira left Chitor and became a wandering mendicant. Many details of her history are obscure, but her marvelous songs have remained as a legacy from her devoted and saintly life. She finally settled in Dwaraka, where, tradition tells us, she entered into final union with her beloved Krishna.

Mira Bai

Today I witnessed the Lord of Beauty—my Girdhar!
Beautiful His form, such as would send a Cupid into ecstasy.
His eyes shot forth captivating rays of effulgence.
He played deftly on the flute as amidst His companions
    He danced to its tune—
Since that moment His sweet Form has taken up its abode
    in my heart, and does not leave me for a moment.
I have surrendered myself and am verily a sacrifice to
    Him, and I lay down at His feet all modesty which the
    world honours.

145

Mira wooes Him, the Beloved of Brindaban, dweller of
*Tulsi-Kunjas,** with all her love.

ॐ

Mine eyes ache for a sight of Thee;
Since Thou has left me, my Lord, I have found no rest,
My bosom heaves at Thy name, so sweet does it sound.
I have fixed my sight on Thy path and await Thy return.
The night seems half a year.
O! to whom shall I recite the tale of the pangs of separation?
My friend, I feel as if the saw is being applied to my eyes.
When wilt Thou meet me, O Lord of Mira—
Thou who bestows joy and allays pain?
For Thee—night after night, I keep vigil and make the
same lament.

ॐ

I pass the night in sleeplessness—counting the hours—
when will the day break?
The moonbeams torture me and the moon like a rapier
frowns, and wakes me from my dream.
Sighing and pining I pass the hours. When will the morning
dawn?
Madness has won me for her own, all consciousness of the
body is gone, who can interpret my feelings?
Only He—the Bestower of Life and Death—can know what
is befalling His Mira!

ॐ

Visit me, Thou—the King of my heart!
I am being consumed in separation from Thee—come slake
my thirst for Thee.
I pass my night in traversing the courtyard over and over
again.
Desire for food and sleep has left me. Why does not
my life-breath forsake me?
Give life to the ailing one, O Lord, by Thy *Darshan* [vision]!

* A grove of trees where Sri Krishna danced and enjoyed the company
of his devotees.

ॐ

For Thy sake, O darling one! I forsook all comforts—
why dost Thou now remain away from me?
My heart is aflame with the fire of Thy separation.
Come Thou and comfort me.
Since it is not possible for me to evade its hold, come
Thou smiling therefore to meet me.
Mira is Thy own—through ages—why dost not Thou come and
embrace her?

ॐ

A suppliant, Lord, I beg of Thee, take me up,
I have suffered much by birth into this world.
Efface the memory and trials of the world.
Remove the bondages created by my activities in lives past,
In the cycle of innumerable existences in this world I
have passed through.
Lord Girdhar, save me from this cycle of transmigration,
begs Mira.

ॐ

I am mad with love and, who can imagine my agony?
I rest on the cross but how can I know sleep?
In the highest heavens my Lord rests! How can I meet Him?
Only he who is like me oppressed can know of my agony,
As jewellers can alone appraise jewels.
Tormented by pain I wander from one wilderness to another,
and can find no doctor to administer to my ailment.
Only when Girdhar plays the physician shall I be healed,
says Mira.[1]

NOTE

1. From Bankey Behari, *Minstrels of God,* Part I (1956).

20. Tukaram

Tukaram (1598–1650) was born in southwest central India in the state of Maharashtra. Although a member of the lowest caste (*sudra*), a farmer without education, Tukaram became one of the greatest masters of the Marathi language. He is famous for his hundreds of *abhangas,* or unbroken hymns, which flow on and on with astonishing beauty and facility. Despite many personal tragedies (his first wife and son died of starvation during a famine), Tukaram praised God, in the form of Sri Krishna, continuously with his intoxicating music. This was Tukaram's most characteristic mode of worship—called *kirtan*—the spontaneous expression of devotion through singing and dancing. He had an unshakable faith in the Name of God. "Sit silent and repeat the Name and I assure you that it will lead to realization," he urged.

Tukaram's own spiritual ascent was frequently filled with frustration and doubt. Then one day, when on the point of suicide, he experienced the divine vision. The joy of God flowed from him in burst after burst of ecstatic songs. "O God, today's gain is indescribable!" he wrote. "Divine joy is seething through my body! Every day to me is now a holy day . . . I know not night from day, the illumination is ceaseless. . . . All houses and palaces have now become the temples of God. Whatever I hear is the name of God."

Tukaram considered ethics and formal religion merely a prelude to the goal of life—which was the bliss of the realization of God. The following songs fully express this aim.

Tukaram

The Form of the Lord

Superior is the worship of the Lord with form;
It is supreme devotion.
Such worship brings one realization
    and every divine experience.
Such worship purifies the heart
And from it emerges the beautiful Lord
In his captivating form.

The Name of the Lord is the seed
And the fruit which springs forth;
It is the highest religion.
It is the essence of all religious practice.
His name banishes all trouble—
For where the devotee chants his name
There all virtues meet.

When the Lord enters the heart
And ascends his throne
All that is good appears there—
And no more does the devotee know
    the pain of rebirth.
Do not, therefore, fear to follow
The faith of your birth.
Repeat His name—that is all one needs.

How many names he has! the Vedas
Call him the perennial Being
The yogis the formless One
And the liberated know him
    as the radiant Atman.
But Tukaram knows him as Krishna
Who, for the sake of his devotee,
    assumed the radiant form of a man.

Am I Condemned?

Though for others the Lord may live,
To me he is dead—
Since he answers not my call.
If I am to be condemned as sinner
(I who contemplate thy lotus feet!)
Then with whom does the blame lie?
Is this sin of mine greater than thy lotus feet?
Had I not been a sinner
How couldst thou have then been my deliverer?
Truly O Compassionate One
My name precedes Thine.[1]

My Heart Cries to Thee

As on the bank the poor fish lies
And gasps and writhes in pain,
Or, as a man with anxious eyes
Seeks hidden gold in vain,
So is my heart distressed, and cries
To come to thee again.

Thou knowest, Lord, the agony
Of the lost infant's wail
Yearning his mother's face to see.
(How oft I tell this tale.)
O, at thy feet the mystery
Of the dark world unveil.

The fire of this harassing thought
Upon my bosom prays.
Why is it I am thus forgot?
(O, who can know thy ways?)
Nay Lord, thou seest my hapless lot;
Have mercy, Tuka says.

I Enjoy Thy Bliss

I saw my death with my own eyes.
Incomparably glorious was the occasion.
The whole universe was filled with joy.
I became everything and enjoyed everything.
I had hitherto clung to only one place,
Being pent up in egotism in this body.
By my deliverance from it,
I am enjoying a harvest of bliss.
Death and birth are now no more.
I am free from the littleness of "me" and "mine."
God has given me a place to live
And I am proclaiming him to the whole world.

N O T E

1. This poem and the preceding revised from Bankey Behari, *Minstrels of God*, part II (1956).

21. Ramprasad

One of the most inspired worshipers of God in the aspect of the
Divine Mother was the Bengali singer of hymns, Ramprasad
(1718-1775). Born at Kumarhati, he was given a good education
in medicine and languages, but it soon became apparent that he
yearned only for the religious life. At practical living he was
a failure. After marrying, he managed to obtain a job as book-
keeper and accountant, but instead of keeping accounts he wrote
hymns to the Divine Mother on the pages of the ledger. When
his employer discovered this, he at once recognized Ramprasad's
genius. Instead of being annoyed, he sent him home with a promise
to support the poet with an allowance for the rest of his life.

In the years to follow, Ramprasad's fame as a singer and
composer spread throughout Bengal. He became a favorite of the
local rajah and was known as the "Entertainer of Poets." It
was Ramprasad's habit to wade into the Ganges up to his neck,
then let his songs to the Mother pour out across the waters.
Boats on the river would stop, and people would gather on the
shore to listen. To this day, his beautiful songs are still sung by
rich and poor, by holy men and schoolboys. And those dying on
the banks of the Ganges often ask to hear a song by Ramprasad.

Ramprasad

Hymns

Come, let us go for a walk, O mind, to Kali, the Wish-
    fulfilling Tree,
And there beneath It gather the four fruits of life.
Of your two wives, Dispassion and Worldliness,

Bring along Dispassion only, on your way to the Tree,
And ask her son Discrimination about the Truth.

When will you learn to lie, O mind, in the abode of
    Blessedness,
With Cleanliness and Defilement on either side of you?
Only when you have found the way
To keep these wives contentedly under a single roof,
Will you behold the matchless form of Mother Shyama.

Ego and Ignorance, your parents, instantly banish from
    your sight;
And should Delusion seek to drag you to its hole,
Manfully cling to the pillar of Patience.
Tie to the post of Unconcern the goats of Vice and Virtue,
Killing them with the sword of Knowledge if they rebel.

With the children of Worldliness, your first wife, plead
    from a goodly distance,
And, if they will not listen, drown them in Wisdom's sea.
Says Ramprasad: If you do as I say,
You can submit a good account, O mind, to the King of Death,
And I shall be well pleased with you and call you my darling.

                          ॐ

In the world's busy market-place, O Shyama, Thou art
    flying kites;
High up they soar on the wind of hope, held fast by
    maya's string.
Their frames are human skeletons, their sails of the
    three gunas made;
But all their curious workmanship is merely for ornament.

Upon the kite-strings Thou hast rubbed the manja paste of
    worldliness,
So as to make each straining strand all the more sharp
    and strong.
Out of a hundred thousand kites, at best but one or two
    break free;
And Thou dost laugh and clap Thy hands, O Mother,
    watching them!

On favouring winds, says Ramprasad, the kites set loose
  will speedily
Be borne away to the Infinite, across the sea of the world.

ॐ

Taking the name of Kali, dive deep down, O mind,
Into the heart's fathomless depths,
Where many a precious gem lies hid.
But never believe the bed of the ocean bare of gems
If in the first few dives you fail;
With firm resolve and self-control
Dive deep and make your way to Mother Kali's realm.
Down in the ocean depths of heavenly Wisdom lie
The wondrous pearls of Peace, O mind;
And you yourself can gather them,
If you but have pure love and follow the scriptures' rule.
Within those ocean depths, as well,
Six alligators lurk—lust, anger, and the rest—
Swimming about in search of prey.
Smear yourself with the turmeric of discrimination;
The very smell of it will shield you from their jaws.

Upon the ocean bed lie strewn
Unnumbered pearls and precious gems;
Plunge in, says Ramprasad, and gather up handfuls there!

ॐ

How are you trying, O my mind, to know the nature of God?
You are groping like a madman locked in a dark room.
He is grasped through ecstatic love; how can you fathom
  Him without it?
Only through affirmation, never negation, can you know Him;
Neither through Veda nor through Tantra nor the six *darshanas*.*

It is in love's elixir only that He delights, O mind;
He dwells in the body's inmost depths, in Everlasting Joy.
And, for that love, the mighty yogis practise yoga from
  age to age;

---

* *darshanas*—the six basic schools of Indian philosophy.

When love awakes, the Lord, like a magnet, draws to Him
    the soul.
He it is, says Ramprasad, that I approach as Mother;
But must I give away the secret, here in the market-place?
From the hints I have given, O mind, guess what that Being is!

ॐ

    O mind, you do not know how to farm!
    Fallow lies the field of your life.
    If you had only worked it well,
    How rich a harvest you might reap!
    Hedge it about with Kali's name
    If you would keep your harvest safe;
    This is the stoutest hedge of all,
    For Death himself cannot come near it.

    Sooner or later will dawn the day
    When you must forfeit your precious field;
    Gather, O mind, what fruit you may.
    Sow for your seed the holy name
    Of God that your guru has given to you,
    Faithfully watering it with love;
    And if you should find the task too hard,
    Call upon Ramprasad for help.[1]

NOTE

1. From Swami Nikhilananda, translator, *The Gospel of Sri Ramakrishna*
(1942).

22. Tulsidas

Tulsidas (1523-1623) did not preach a new doctrine or found a religious sect, but the example of his life and the genius of his poetry have established him as one of India's great teachers. Very little is known of his early years, except that he was orphaned when still a young boy and forced to wander the streets in search of food and shelter. However, he was adopted by a *sadhu* by the name of Naraharidasa, who was told in a dream to find the boy and instruct him in the teachings of Rama. Naraharidasa did as he was urged and later became Tulsidas's *guru*.

As Tulsidas learned the story of Rama and listened enraptured to the beautiful verses of the *Ramayana,* he felt compelled to glorify Rama with his own poetry. The result was more than a dozen works in either praise or interpretation of his Chosen Ideal. Perhaps the most famous of these is the *Ramacaritamanasa* or life story of Rama, which greatly helped to revitalize the faith of the people in their own culture, a faith which had been badly shaken by the Moslem rule. Tulsidas also endeared himself to the common man by writing in his native language rather than Sanskrit.

Tulsidas had that rare ability to make God distinctly human. He showed through his verses that the Godhead of nondualistic Vedanta, the formless Brahman, is the same as the Godhead in human form worshiped by the devotee. "How is the unqualified, the qualified also? As water is identical with ice and hail-stone." He considered the power of the Name invincible.

The selections to follow come from *The Petition to Ram* or *Vinyapartika,* which some scholars have compared to the Book of Psalms. It is a collection of 279 devotional hymns of supplication, self-revelation, and praise. From a number of them we are also granted a glimpse into Tulsidas's own life; thus this work remains one of the few biographical references available.

Tulsidas

The Letter of Petition

You are merciful and I am poor,
   You are bountiful and I a beggar,
I am a famous sinner,
   You drive away many sins;
You are master of the masterless,
   And who is more masterless than I?
No other is so afflicted as I,
   Nor banisher of afflictions as you;
You are Brahma* and I am a soul,
   You are overlord and I your slave,
You are father, mother, teacher,
   Comrade, in every way my benefactor;
Yours and mine are many bonds,
   Own whichever please you!
So that Tulsi by any means, O compassionate,
   May gain the shelter of your feet.

ॐ

Up till now I've wasted *time*—now I'll waste no more!
Through Ram's grace the night of existence has passed, and
   now that I'm awake I'll make my bed no more!
I have found the beauteous philosopher's stone—that Name,
   I'll not let it go again from out my heart-hands!
And with the touchstone of that pure, dark, lovely form, I'll
   get my heart's gold tested!
Knowing me to be beneath the dominance of others—the
   objects of this world—these senses made mock of me, but
   since I'm my own master, I'll not be their laughing-stock.
Tulsi takes this vow: that his mind's bee shall forever
   dwell by Raghupati's lotus-feet.

* *Brahma*—a reference to Brahman, The Impersonal Godhead, not
Brahma, the Creator–God of the Hindu trinity.

Without love for such a dear one as Ram a creature lives in
vain,
That pleasure which you regard as pleasure, understand how
much it is indeed pleasure!
Wherever in whatever womb you have taken birth, in heaven,
earth or hell,
There you have sought out the pleasures of the senses, and—
as it was ordained—obtained them.
Why are you ensnared by delusion and absorbed in stitching
up the torn heavens?
Says Tulsi, why do you not sing the goodly praises of the
Lord, and drink of the nectar *of devotion?*

ॐ

When shall I live in such a wise
That by compassionate Raghunath's* mercy I shall grasp the
nature of a saint?
Satisfied with what may come, never wishing anything of any,
Ever absorbed in doing good to others, shall I keep that
rule by thought, word and deed;
Hearing with my ears most unbearable, harsh words, I shall
not burn with their fire,
But with pride banished and a cool level mind, I shall
count others' virtues, not their vices:
Giving up the anxieties which arise from body, I shall
bear pleasure and pain with equanimity,
And, Lord, I—Tulsi Das—remaining in this path shall
obtain unwavering devotion to Hari.[1]

Some Sayings of Tulsidas

Someone once asked Tulsidas what was the surest and swiftest
way to realization. He replied: "If you will constantly repeat the
Lord's name, with no hope of reward, so that you lose consciousness while chanting it, you shall obtain the supreme gift."

Once Jahangir, a powerful king, asked Tulsidas to perform
a miracle. The saint answered: "Miracle-mongering is not the pro-

* *Raghunath*—a name of Rama.

fession of the sage; it is a trickster's job. A *dervish's* devotion suffers if he indulges in such acts. If a true devotee persists in performing miracles, he shall be deprived of the vision of the Lord."

Once Jahangir offered Tulsidas a heavy purse of money. Tulsidas replied: "One who wants to perform the Lord's devotion, should never seek to accumulate riches. The contemplation of money and its attendant anxieties soil the mind and render it unfit for meditation upon the Lord."

A raja (Tilak Singh) once asked Tulsidas to confer upon him undivided devotion to God. Tulsidas said to him: "Not until the taste for sensual delights of this world is banished can man taste the joys of eternity. You must give up the company of the worldly, your courtiers and flatterers—for they are a prey to sensual objects. On hearing such matters the mind begins to dwell upon them and this leads us to a spiritual fall. If you wish to love God, give up the company of worldly people immediately. Your courtiers, by their sweet talk, forget the fetters of *rajas* [passion], *tamas* [dullness]—and these bind you. If you desire to realize your aim retire to the wilderness . . . and dwell among the saints. Their company, even for a moment, will pave the way to realization."[2]

NOTES

1. From F. R. Allchin, translator, *Tulsi Das: The Petition to Ram* (a translation of *Vinaya-patrika*) (1966).
2. From Bankey Behari, *Minstrels of God*, Part II (1956).

V

THE HINDU RENAISSANCE

23. Sri Ramakrishna

Sri Ramakrishna (1836-1886) is unquestionably the most significant spiritual personality to emerge from India in the past several hundred years. Although the saintliness of Ramakrishna is sufficiently inspiring in itself, his greatest contribution was to demonstrate through the example of his life and teachings the underlying unity of all religions. Such an idea, of course, is not new to India, for Hinduism has never been exclusively narrow or dogmatic. But in Ramakrishna the concept of universality found a comprehensive and meaningful embodiment, through his practice of the disciplines of other faiths and his mystical experience of their truths. As a spiritual teacher, Ramakrishna belonged to neither caste nor country, but was a universal figure of heroic proportions whom all spiritual aspirants may claim as a modern interpreter of their own particular faith.

The details of his life, like those of many other men of God, were extremely simple and unpretentious. He was born Gadadhar Chattopadhyaya in Kamarpukur, a small village near Calcutta. During his early years, his boyish charm and innocence were immensely attractive to all who knew him. He was talented at mimicry and painting. At the age of sixteen, he joined his brother Ramkumar, who had begun a Sanskrit school in Calcutta; after a few years, he began to assist Ramkumar in his new duties as priest of the Kali temple at nearby Dakshineswar. It was here that Ramakrishna was to spend the remainder of his life, undergoing severe spiritual disciplines, meditating on the Divine Mother, and patiently teaching the many hundreds of devotees who came to him for instructions.

The final five years of Ramakrishna's life were, in many ways, the most important. During these years his disciples and devotees, many of whom would carry forth his message, began to gather about him. The story of these years is told in the *Sri Sri Rama-krishna Kathamrita (Gospel of Sri Ramakrishna),* written by one of his householder disciples, Mahendranath Gupta (who referred to himself simply as "M."), and it is from this book that the selections to follow are taken. The *Gospel* is a unique book which presents with stenographic accuracy the utterances, activities, and spiritual revelations of one of the great saints of modern times.

Sri Ramakrishna

The First Meeting

The temple of Mother Kali is on the bank of the Ganges at Dakshineswar. It was here in February 1882, a few days after the birthday celebration of Sri Ramakrishna, that M. met him.

While out visiting several other gardens, M. and his friend Sidhu happened to arrive at the temple garden of Dakshineswar. It was Sunday. A few minutes previously, while they were walking in the garden of Prasanna Bannerji, Sidhu had said, "There is a beautiful garden on the bank of the Ganges. Would you care to visit it? A holy man, a paramahamsa, lives there."

Entering through the main gateway of the temple, both M. and Sidhu went straight to Sri Ramakrishna's room.

M. found Sri Ramakrishna seated on the wooden couch, facing east. With a smile on his face, he was talking of God. The devotees were sitting on the floor. The room was crowded. In silence, they were drinking the nectar of his words.

M. stood there speechless. It seemed to him as if Shukadeva* himself were teaching the wisdom of God; as if all the holy places had come together, as it were, in this very room. Or as if Sri Chaitanya himself, with his devotees Ramananda, Swarup and the rest, were singing the praises of the Lord as they sat in Puri, the sacred city.

Sri Ramakrishna was saying: "When a man sheds tears and when his hair stands on end if he utters the name of Hari or Rama

---

* The narrator of the *Bhagavata Purana* and son of Vyasa; regarded as one of India's ideal monks.

even once, then you may know for certain that he no longer needs to perform any rituals. Then only does he have the right to renounce them—or rather, they themselves will drop away from him. Then it will be enough merely to chant the name of Rama or Hari, or just the Word Om." Continuing, he said: "Ritualistic worship becomes merged in the sacred Gayatri mantra; and the Gayatri likewise becomes merged in Om."

As M. looked on in wonder, he thought to himself, "Ah, what a fascinating place! And what a fascinating man! I don't want to leave this place." But then, after a while, he thought, "I'll take a look around first and find out exactly where I am. Then I'll come back and sit here."

When M. and Sidhu left the room, they could hear the sweet music of the vesper service, made by gong, bell, drum, and cymbals, combined. Sweet music also issued from the *nahabat* at the south end of the garden. The sounds of music seemed to roll away over the bosom of the Ganges and become lost in the distance. A soft spring wind was whispering, laden with the fragrance of flowers. The moon had just risen. It was as if nature in all her aspects were preparing for the evening worship. M. took part in the vespers which were held in the twelve Shiva temples, the Radhakanta Temple and the Temple of Mother Kali, and his heart was filled with great joy. Sidhu remarked, "This temple garden was founded by Rani Rasmani. Regular services are held in all the temples here. Many holy men and beggars are fed here every day."

Talking thus, M. and Sidhu walked across the temple courtyard from the Temple of Mother Kali, and reached the door of Sri Ramakrishna's room. This time, they found the door shut.

M. had been trained in the manners of the English; he would not enter a room unannounced. Brinda, a maidservant, was standing by the door. M. addressed her, "Hello! Is the Holy Man in there now?" Brinda answered, "Yes, he's in there."

M.

How long has he been living here?

Brinda

Oh—many years.

M.

Does he study a great number of books?

Brinda

Books? Oh dear, no! They're all on his tongue.

M. was fresh from the university. He was amazed to learn that Sri Ramakrishna was not a scholar.

M.

Perhaps he is now engaged in his evening worship? Is it possible for us to go in? Will you please get his permission for us to see him?

Brinda

Go right in, children. Just go in and sit down.

When they entered the room, they found Sri Ramakrishna sitting alone on the wooden couch. Incense was burning and all the doors were shut. As he came in, M. saluted the Master with folded hands. The Master asked them to be seated. M. and Sidhu sat down on the floor. Sri Ramakrishna asked them, "Where do you live? What's your occupation? Why have you come to Baranagore?" and similar questions. M. introduced himself by answering all these questions, but he noticed that the Master became absent-minded from time to time. Later he learned that this mood is called *bhava* (ecstasy). This attitude of mind is like that of a fisherman who sits rod in hand, fishing. The float bobs up and down, for a fish has swallowed the bait. He watches the float with eagerness and concentration. At this time, he will speak to no one. Such was Sri Ramakrishna's state of mind. Later, M. not only heard but observed for himself how Sri Ramakrishna would enter into this mood after dusk. Then, again, he would sometimes lose outer consciousness altogether.

M.

Would you like to perform your evening worship, now? Should we take leave of you?

Sri Ramakrishna

(*Still in ecstasy*) No. Evening worship? No, it is not that.

After some further conversation, M. saluted the Master and took leave of him. Sri Ramakrishna said, "Come again."

On his way home, M. began to think, "Who is this serene-looking man? How I wish I could go back to him! Is it possible for a man to be great without being a scholar? How amazing! I want to see him again. And he himself asked me to come again. I shall go to him either tomorrow morning, or the day after."

[*A few days later M. visits Sri Ramakrishna for the second time. They exchange a few pleasantries. Then Ramakrishna begins to question M. about his personal life:*]

Sri Ramakrishna

(*To M.*) Are you married?

M.

Yes, sir.

Sri Ramakrishna

(*Shuddering*) Oh, Ramlal, what a shame! He is married!

Ramlal was a nephew of Sri Ramakrishna and was employed as a priest in the Kali Temple. M. was confused and sat hanging his head in silence, like one who is guilty of a grave crime. He thought to himself, "What is wrong in getting married?"

Then the Master asked, "Have you any children?"

M's heart was beating fast. He said nervously, "Yes, sir, I have children."

The Master became very sad on hearing this and exclaimed, "What a shame! He even has children!"

Thus rebuked, M. remained speechless. His pride began to be humbled. After a few moments, Sri Ramakrishna looked at him graciously and said to him in a kind tone, "You see, you have certain auspicious signs which I recognize by looking at your forehead, eyes, and so forth. . . . Tell me, what kind of a woman is your wife? Does she possess power for good or power for evil?"

M.

She is a good woman, sir, but she's ignorant.

Sri Ramakrishna

(*Cuttingly*) And you're a wise man, are you?

M. did not yet know what constitutes knowledge and what constitutes ignorance. He supposed that a person who is educated and who studies books acquires knowledge. Later on, this misconception was corrected. For he learned that knowledge is to know God and that ignorance is not to know God. When the Master asked, "And you're a wise man, are you?" M's ego received a severe blow.

Sri Ramakrishna

Tell me, do you believe in God with form or without form?

M. was surprised and said to himself, "If one believes that God has form, how can one believe that God is without form? Or again, if a man believes in a formless God, how can he believe in a God with form? Can two contradictory ideas both be true? Can milk be white and black at the same time?"

M.

Sir, I like to believe in God without form.

Sri Ramakrishna

That's good. It's enough to have faith in one aspect of God. You have faith in God without form. That is very good. But never get it into your head that your faith alone is true and that every other is false. Know for certain that God without form is real and that God with form is also real. Then hold fast to whichever faith appeals to you.

M. was amazed to hear that both these ideas could be true. This was something beyond his book-learning. His ego had received a third blow. But, since it was not yet completely crushed, he was ready to continue the argument with the Master.

M.

But, sir, assuming it is true that God has form, he is surely not identical with the clay image of him?

Sri Ramakrishna

Why say that the image is clay? The image is composed of spirit.

M. could not understand what was meant by an "image composed of spirit."

M.

But those who worship the clay image should be made to understand that the clay image is not God, and that while they are bowing down before the image they must remember that they are worshipping God. They must not worship the clay.

Sri Ramakrishna

(*Sharply*) Making others understand—giving them lectures—that's all you Calcutta people think about! You never ask yourselves how *you* can find the truth. Who are *you* to teach others? It is the Lord of the Universe who teaches mankind. Will he who has done so much for us fail to bring us to the light? If we need to be taught, he will teach. He knows our inmost thoughts.

Supposing it *is* a mistake to worship God in the image—doesn't he know he alone is being worshipped? He will certainly be pleased by that worship. Why should *you* get a headache over that? It would be better if you struggled to get knowledge and devotion, yourself.

This time, M. felt that his pride was completely crushed. M. said to himself, "What he says is very true. Who am I to teach others? Have I known God? Do I even have any devotion to him? I am like a man who has no bed to lie on, and yet invites a stranger to share it with him. I do not know God, nor have I heard much about him. How shameful, how utterly foolish of me to think that I can teach others about God! This is not like mathematics, or history, or literature—those one can teach to others. This is the truth of God—the only Reality. . . . I like what the Master says." This was his first argument with the Master and also his last.

Sri Ramakrishna

You were talking of worshipping a clay image. Even if it is made of clay, there is a need for that sort of worship. God himself has arranged for many ways of worship to suit the varied temperaments of his worshippers in their different stages of growth.

A mother has five children. There is fish to be cooked. She prepares different kinds of fish dishes, to agree with every kind of stomach. For one child, she cooks fish pilau, for another pickled fish, for another baked fish, fried fish and so forth. She has cooked all kinds of dishes to appeal to their different tastes and digestions. Do you follow me?

M.

Yes, sir. (*Humbly*) How can we devote our minds to God?

Sri Ramakrishna

Chant the name of God and sing his glories unceasingly; and keep holy company. Now and then one should visit holy men and devotees of God. If a man lives in the world and busies himself day and night with worldly duties and responsibilities, he cannot give his mind to God. So it's important to go into solitude from time to time, and think about God. When the plant is young, it should be fenced on all sides. Unless there's a fence around it, goats and cattle may eat it up.

When you meditate, go into the solitude of a forest, or a quiet corner, and enter into the chamber of your heart. And always keep your power of discrimination awake. God alone is real, that is to say, eternal; everything else is unreal, because it will pass away. As you discriminate in this manner, let your mind give up its attachment to the fleeting objects of this world.

M.

(*Humbly*) How is one to live in the world and lead a family life?

Sri Ramakrishna

Attend to all your duties but keep your mind fixed on God. Wife, son, father, mother—live with all of them and serve them, as if they were your very own. But know in your heart of hearts that they are not your own.

The maid in the house of a rich man attends to her work, but her mind dwells in her home in her native village. Furthermore, she brings up her master's children as though they were her own. She speaks of them as "my Rama" or "my Hari," but she knows in her own mind that they do not belong to her. The tortoise moves about in the water of a lake. But do you know where her mind is? On the bank, where her eggs are laid. Do all your duties in the world, but let your mind dwell on thoughts of God. If you enter into family life before you have cultivated love for God, you will get more and more entangled. You will not be able to face and withstand the attack of dangers, griefs, and sorrows. And the more you think of the objects of the world, the more you will become attached to them.

Before you break open a jack fruit you must rub your hands with oil, otherwise the gummy juice of the fruit will stick to them. Anoint yourself with love for God, and then you can attend to the duties of the world.

But to develop this love of God, one must live in solitude. To make butter, the milk must first be curdled in a secluded spot. If you stir up the milk, it does not curdle. You must stop all your other tasks, and sit down quietly and churn the curd. Then only will you get butter.

If you apply your mind to meditation on the Lord in solitude and silence, you will acquire dispassion, knowledge and devotion to the Lord. But if you give up your mind to worldly thoughts, it becomes degraded. In the world, the only thoughts are of lust and greed.

The world may be likened to water and the mind to milk. If you pour milk into water, they mingle, and the pure milk can no longer be found. But if you first curdle the milk and churn the curd into butter, you can put it into water and it will float. So you must first practise spiritual disciplines and obtain the butter of knowledge and devotion. This cannot be contaminated by the water of the world. It will float, as it were.

At the same time, keep your power of discrimination active. One enjoys lust and gold for a while only. God alone is eternal.

Money—what can it give you? Food, clothes and a place to live in, that's all. It cannot help you to realize God. So money can't be the goal of life. . . . This is what's known as practising discrimination. Do you follow me?

M.

Yes, sir. . . . Sir, can one see God?

Sri Ramakrishna

Most certainly you can! And this is what you must do in order to see him: live in solitude from time to time. Chant the name of the Lord and his glories. And discriminate between the eternal and non-eternal.

M.

What state of mind makes a man able to see God?

Sri Ramakrishna

Cry to him with a yearning heart, and you will see him. Men weep a jugful of tears for their wives and children. And for money they shed enough tears to flood a river. But who weeps for God? Seek him with a loving heart.

Having said this, the Master sang:

Seek Mother Shyama, O my mind,
    With a longing heart,
    With a yearning heart,
She will not withhold herself.
For how can the Mother withhold herself?
How can Kali the Mother withhold her presence?

Sri Ramakrishna continued: "Yearning for God is like the coming of dawn. Dawn comes before the sun itself rises. When yearning for God comes, the vision of God himself must follow.

"The worldly man loves his wealth; the mother loves her child; the chaste wife loves her husband. If your love for God is as intense as all these three attachments put together, then you will see God.

"Call on God with a longing heart. The kitten simply calls its mother, crying "mew, mew." It stays wherever the mother cat puts it. It doesn't know what else to do. And when the mother cat hears its cry, no matter where she may be, she runs to the kitten."[1]

Conversation with Bankim Chandra

Sri Ramakrishna arrived at Adhar's house with his attendants. Everyone was in a joyous mood. Adhar had arranged a rich feast. Many strangers were present. At Adhar's invitation, several other deputy magistrates had come; they wanted to watch the Master and judge his holiness. Among them was Bankim Chandra Chatterji, perhaps the greatest literary figure of Bengal during the later part of the nineteenth century. He was one of the creators of modern Bengali literature and wrote on social and religious subjects. Bankim was a product of the contact of India with England. He gave modern interpretations of the Hindu scriptures and advocated drastic social reforms.

Sri Ramakrishna had been talking happily with the devotees when Adhar introduced several of his personal friends to him.

Adhar

(Introducing Bankim) Sir, he is a great scholar and has written many books. He has come here to see you. His name is Bankim Babu.

Master

(Smiling) Bankim!* Well, what has made you bent?

Bankim

(Smiling) Why, sir, boots are responsible for it. The kicks of our white masters have bent my body.

Master

No, my dear sir! Sri Krishna was bent on account of His ecstatic love. His body was bent in three places owing to His love for Radha. That is how some people explain Sri Krishna's

* Literally the word means "bent" or "curved."

form. Do you know why He has a deep-blue complexion? And why He is of such small stature—only three and a half cubits measured by His own hand? God looks so as long as He is seen from a distance. So the water of the ocean looks blue from afar. But if you go near the ocean and take the water in your hand, you will no longer find it blue; it will be very clear, transparent. So the sun appears small because it is very far away; if you go near it, you will no longer find it small. When one knows the true nature of God, He appears neither blue nor small. But that is a far-off vision: one does not see it except in samadhi. As long as "I" and "you" exist, name and form will also exist. Everything is God's lila, His sportive pleasure. As long as a man is conscious of "I" and "you," he will experience the manifestations of God through diverse forms. . . .

As Sri Ramakrishna finished these words, Bankim and his friends began to whisper in English.

Master

(*Smiling, to Bankim and the others*) Well, gentlemen! What are you talking about in English?

Adhar

We are discussing what you have just said, your explanation of Krishna's form.

Master

(*Smiling*) That reminds me of a funny story. It makes me want to laugh. Once a barber was shaving a gentleman. The latter was cut slightly by the razor. At once he cried out, "Damn!" But the barber didn't know the meaning of the word. He put his razor and other shaving articles aside, tucked up his shirt-sleeves—it was winter, and said: "You said 'damn' to me. Now you must tell me its meaning." The gentleman said: "Don't be silly. Go on with your shaving. The word doesn't mean anything in particular; but shave a little more carefully." But the barber wouldn't let him off so easily. He said, "If 'damn' means something good, then I am a 'damn,' my father is a 'damn,' and all my ancestors are 'damns.'" (*All laugh.*) But if it means something bad, then you are a 'damn,' your father is a 'damn,' and all your ancestors are 'damns.' (*All laugh.*) They are not only 'damns,' but 'damn—damn—damn—da-damn—damn.' " *(Loud Laughter.)*

As the laughter stopped, Bankim began the conversation.

Bankim

Sir, why don't you preach?

Master

(*Smiling*) Preaching? It is only a man's vanity that makes him think of preaching. A man is but an insignificant creature. It is God alone who will preach—God who has created the sun and moon and so illumined the universe. Is preaching such a trifling affair? You cannot preach unless God reveals Himself to you and gives you the command to preach. Of course, no one can stop you from preaching. You haven't received the command, but still you cry yourself hoarse. People will listen to you a couple of days and then forget all about it. It is like any other sensation: as long as you speak, people will say, "Ah! He speaks well"; and the moment you stop, everything will disappear.

The milk in the pot hisses and swells as long as there is heat under it. Take away the heat, and the milk will quiet down as before.

One must increase one's strength by *sadhana;* otherwise one cannot preach. As the proverb goes: "You have no room to sleep yourself and you invite a friend to sleep with you." There is no place for you to lie down and you say: "Come, friend! Come and lie down with me." (*Laughter.*)

Some people used to befoul the bank of the Haldarpukur* at Kamarpukur every morning. The villagers would notice it and abuse the offenders. But that didn't stop it. At last the villagers filed a petition with the government. An officer visited the place and put up a sign: "Commit no nuisance. Offenders will be punished." That stopped it completely. Afterwards there was no more trouble. It was a government order, and everyone had to obey it.

Likewise, if God reveals Himself to you and gives you the

---

* A small lake near Ramakrishna's birthplace.

command, then you can preach and teach people. Otherwise, who will listen to you? *(The visitors were listening seriously.)*

Master

(To Bankim) I understand you are a great pundit and have written many books. Please tell me what you think about man's duties? What will accompany him after death? You believe in the hereafter, don't you?

Bankim

The hereafter? What is that?

Master

True. When a man dies after attaining Knowledge, he doesn't have to go to another plane of existence; he isn't born again. But as long as he has not attained Knowledge, as long as he has not realized God, he must come back to the life of this earth; he can never escape it. For such a person there is a hereafter. A man is liberated after attaining Knowledge, after realizing God. For him there is no further coming back to earth. If a boiled paddy-grain is sown, it doesn't sprout. Just so, if a man is boiled by the fire of Knowledge, he cannot take part any more in the play of creation; he cannot lead a worldly life, for he has no attachment to "woman and gold."* What will you gain by sowing boiled paddy?

Bankim

(Smiling) Sir, neither does a weed serve the purpose of a tree.

Master

But you cannot call a *jnani* a weed. He who has realized God has obtained the fruit of Immortality—not a common fruit like a gourd or a pumpkin. He is free from rebirth. He is not born anywhere—on earth, in the solar world, or in the lunar world.

---

* The term "woman and gold" (*kaminikanchana*) is a favorite expression of Ramakrishna. By it he meant "lust and greed"—the two chief impediments to spiritual progress. When speaking to women devotees, he advised them to shun "man." Sri Ramakrishna never taught anyone to hate woman or womankind, but rather to regard them as images of the Divine Mother. But he warned against immersing oneself in sensuality, and pointed out its dangers time and time again.

Analogy is one-sided. You are a pundit; haven't you read logic? Suppose you say that a man is as terrible as a tiger. That doesn't mean that he has a fearful tail or a tiger's pot-face! (*All laugh.*)

I said the same thing to Keshab. He asked me, "Sir, is there an after-life?" I didn't commit myself either way. I said that the potters put their pots in the sun to bake. Among them you see both baked and soft pots. Sometimes cattle trample over them. When the baked pots are broken, the potters throw them away; but when the soft ones are broken they keep them. They mix them with water and put the clay on the wheel and make new pots. They don't throw away the unbaked pots. So I said to Keshab: "The Potter won't let you go as long as you are unbaked. He will put you on the wheel of the world as long as you have not attained Knowledge, as long as you have not realized Him. He won't let you go. You will have to return to the earth again and again: there is no escape. You will be liberated only when you realize God. Then alone will the Potter let you go. It is because then you won't serve any purpose in this world of maya." The jnani has gone beyond maya. What will he do in this world of maya?

But God keeps some jnanis in the world of maya to be teachers of men. In order to teach others the jnani lives in the world with the help of vidyamaya. It is God Himself who keeps the jnani in the world for His work. Such was the case with Shukadeva and Shankaracharya.

(*To Bankim, smiling*) Well, what do you say about man's duties?

Bankim

(*Smiling*) If you ask me about them, I should say they are eating, sleeping, and sex-life.

Master

(*Sharply*) Eh? You are very saucy! What you do day and night comes out through your mouth. A man belches what he eats. If he eats radish, he belches radish; if he eats green coconut, he belches green coconut. Day and night you live in the midst of "woman and gold"; so your mouth utters words about that alone.

By constantly thinking of worldly things a man becomes calculating and deceitful. On the other hand, he becomes guileless by thinking of God. A man who has seen God will never say what you have just said. What will a pundit's scholarship profit him if he does not think of God and has no discrimination and renunciation? Of what use is erudition if the mind dwells on "woman and gold"?

Kites and vultures soar very high indeed, but their gaze is fixed only on the charnel-pit. The pundit has no doubt studied many books and scriptures; he may rattle off their texts, or he may have written books. But if he is attached to women, if he thinks of money and honour as the essential things, will you call him a pundit? How can a man be a pundit if his mind does not dwell on God?

Some may say about the devotees: "Day and night these people speak about God. They are crazy; they have lost their heads. But how clever we are! How we enjoy pleasure—money, honour, the senses!" The crow, too, thinks he is a clever bird; but the first thing he does when he wakes up in the early morning is to fill his stomach with nothing but others' filth. Haven't you noticed how he struts about? Very clever indeed!

(*There was dead silence. Sri Ramakrishna continued*) But like the swan are those who think of God, who pray day and night to get rid of their attachment to worldly things and their love for "woman and gold," who do not enjoy anything except the nectar of the Lotus Feet of the Lord, and to whom worldly pleasures taste bitter. If you put a mixture of milk and water before the swan, it will leave the water and drink only the milk. And haven't you noticed the gait of a swan? It goes straight ahead in one direction. So it is with genuine devotees: they go toward God alone. They seek nothing else; they enjoy nothing else.

(*Tenderly, to Bankim*) Please don't take offense at my words.

Bankim

Sir, I haven't come here to hear sweet things.

Master

(*To Bankim*) "Woman and gold" alone is the world; that alone is maya. Because of it you cannot see or think of God. After the birth of one or two children, husband and wife should live as brother and sister and talk only of God. Then both their minds will be drawn to God, and the wife will be a help to the husband on the path of spirituality. None can taste divine bliss without giving up his animal feeling. A devotee should pray to God to help him get rid of this feeling. It must be a sincere prayer. God is our Inner Controller; He will certainly listen to our prayer if it is sincere.

And "gold." Sitting on the bank of the Ganges below the Panchavati, I used to say, "Rupee is clay and clay is rupee." Then I threw both into the Ganges.

Bankim

Indeed! Money is clay! Sir, if you have a few pennies you can help the poor. If money is clay, then a man cannot give in charity or do good to others.

Master

(*To Bankim*) Charity! Doing good! How dare you say you can do good to others? Man struts about so much; but if one pours foul water into his mouth when he is asleep, he doesn't even know it; his mouth overflows with it. Where are his boasting, his vanity, his pride, then? . . .

If a householder gives in charity in a spirit of detachment, he is really doing good to himself and not to others. It is God alone that he serves—God, who dwells in all beings; and when he serves God, he is really doing good to himself and not to others. If a man thus serves God through all beings, not through men alone but through animals and other living beings as well; if he doesn't seek name and fame, or heaven after death; if he doesn't seek any return from those he serves; if he can carry on his work of service in this spirit—then he performs truly selfless work, work without attachment. Through such selfless work he does good to himself. This is called karmayoga. This too is a way to realize God. But it is very difficult, and not suited to the Kaliyuga.

Therefore I say, he who works in such a detached spirit—who is kind and charitable—benefits only himself. Helping others, doing good to others—this is the work of God alone, who for men has created the sun and moon, father and mother, fruits, flowers, and corn. The love that you see in parents is God's love: He has given it to them to preserve His creation. The compassion that you see in the kind-hearted is God's compassion: He has given it to them to protect the helpless. Whether you are charitable or not, He will have His work done somehow or other. Nothing can stop His work.

What then is man's duty? What else can it be? It is just to take refuge in God and to pray to Him with a yearning heart for His vision. . . .

One must have for God the yearning of a child. The child sees nothing but confusion when his mother is away. You may try to cajole him by putting a sweetmeat in his hand; but he will not be fooled. He only says, "No, I want to go to my mother." One must feel such yearning for God. Ah, what yearning! How restless a child feels for his mother! Nothing can make him forget his mother. He to whom the enjoyment of worldly happiness appears tasteless, he who takes no delight in anything of the world—money, name, creature comforts, sense pleasure, becomes sincerely grief-stricken for the vision of the Mother. And to him alone the Mother comes running, leaving all Her other duties.

Ah, that restlessness is the whole thing. Whatever path you follow—whether you are a Hindu, a Mussalman, a Christian, a Shakta, a Vaishnava, or a Brahmo—the vital point is restlessness. God is our Inner Guide. It doesn't matter if you take a wrong path—only you must be restless for Him. He Himself will put you on the right path.

Besides, there are errors in all paths. Everyone thinks his watch is right; but as a matter of fact no watch is absolutely right. But that doesn't hamper one's work. If a man is restless for God he gains the company of sadhus and as far as possible corrects his own watch with the sadhus' help. . . .

Bankim

(*To the Master*) Sir, how can one develop divine love?

Master

Through restlessness—the restlessness a child feels for his mother. The child feels bewildered when he is separated from his mother, and weeps longingly for her. If a man can weep like that for God he can even see Him.

At the approach of dawn the eastern horizon becomes red. Then one knows it will soon be sunrise. Likewise, if you see a person restless for God, you can be pretty certain that he hasn't long to wait for His vision.

A disciple asked his teacher, "Sir, please tell me how I can see God." "Come with me," said the guru, "and I shall show you." He took the disciple to a lake, and both of them got into the water. Suddenly the teacher pressed the disciple's head under the water. After a few moments he released him and the disciple raised his head and stood up. The guru asked him, "How did you feel?" The disciple said, "Oh! I thought I should die; I was panting for breath." The teacher said, "When you feel like that for God, then you will know you haven't long to wait for His vision."

(To Bankim) Let me tell you something. What will you gain by floating on the surface? Dive a little under the water. The gems lie deep under the water; so what is the good of throwing your arms and legs about on the surface? A real gem is heavy. It doesn't float; it sinks to the bottom. To get the real gem you must dive deep.

Bankim

Sir, what can we do? We are tied to a cork. It prevents us from diving. (All laugh.)

Master

All sins vanish if one only remembers God. His name breaks the fetters of death. You must dive; otherwise you can't get the gem.[2]

NOTES

1. From The Gospel of Sri Ramakrishna, Chap. 1, translated by Swami Prabhavananda and Christopher Isherwood in Christopher Isherwood, Ramakrishna and His Disciples (1965), pp. 258-260; 262-267.

2. From Swami Nikhilananda, translator, The Gospel of Sri Ramakrishna, Chap. 34 (1942), pp. 666-671.

24. Swami Vivekananda

Swami Vivekananda (1863–1902), the leading disciple of Sri Ramakrishna, possessed that rare combination of intellectual brilliance and spiritual attainment which enabled him to carry out his task as Ramakrishna's chief apostle to the West. Born as Narendranath Datta in Calcutta, Vivekananda first met Ramakrishna when only eighteen years of age. Even at this first meeting, Ramakrishna recognized in him the seeds of greatness; he knew that this young man would be a fitting bearer of his spiritual message to the world.

The opportunity came in 1893, when Vivekananda, now a monk, arrived in the United States as a delegate to the Parliament of Religions in Chicago. His success was immediate. For the next seven years Vivekananda lectured, conducted classes in religion, and laid the groundwork for the monastic order which now bears the name of his teacher (the Ramakrishna Math and Mission).

During a return visit to India in 1897, Vivekananda devoted himself to founding the Ramakrishna Mission, which today actively maintains schools, dispensaries, and hospitals throughout India. He returned to the West in 1899, but remained only until the following year. However, the inspiration of his indomitable spirit and zeal for reform was felt by others, who continued to carry on his teachings. Because of Vivekananda's work, twelve Vedanta centers are now active in the United States.

Vivekananda was a brilliant orator, and his published works are, to a large extent, the edited transcripts of his lectures in the United States and England. The first two selections included here are from two of his major lectures. "The Ideal of a Universal Religion" was delivered on January 12, 1896, in New York; "Practical Vedanta" was given in London, November 10 of the same year. The selections from *Inspired Talks* reveal a Vivekananda away from the lecture platform, working with a small group of disciples that had invited him to spend the summer of 1895 at a house in Thousand Island Park in upstate New York. In many ways, these teachings remain some of his most inspired flashes of wisdom.

Swami Vivekananda

From *The Ideal of a Universal Religion*

Religion is the highest plane of human thought and life, and herein we find that the workings of these two forces have been most marked. The intensest love that humanity has ever known has come from religion, and the most diabolical hatred that humanity has known has also come from religion. The noblest words of peace that the world has ever heard have come from men on the religious plane, and the bitterest denunciation that the world has ever known has been uttered by religious men. The higher the goal of any religion and the finer its organization, the more remarkable are its activities. No other human motive has deluged the world with so much blood as religion; at the same time, nothing has brought into existence so many hospitals and asylums for the poor, no other human influence has taken such care, not only of humanity, but also of the lowest of animals, as religion. Nothing makes us so cruel as religion, and nothing makes us so tender as religion. This has been so in the past and will also, in all probability, be so in the future.

Yet out of the midst of this din and turmoil, this strife and struggle, this hatred and jealousy of religions and sects, there have arisen, from time to time, potent voices drowning all this noise —making themselves heard from pole to pole, as it were—proclaiming peace and harmony.

Will it ever come? Is it possible that there should ever reign unbroken harmony in this plane of mighty religious struggle? The world is exercised in the latter part of this century by the question of harmony. In society various plans are being proposed, and attempts are made to carry them into practice. But we know how difficult it is to do so. People find that it is almost impossible to mitigate the fury of the struggle of life, to tone down the tremendous nervous tension that is in man. Now, if it is so difficult to bring harmony and peace on the physical plane of life—the external and gross side of it—then it must be a thousand times more difficult to bring harmony and peace to rule over the internal nature of man.

I would ask you for the time being to come out of the network of words. We have all been hearing from childhood of such things as love, peace, charity, equality, and universal brotherhood; but they have become to us mere words without meaning, words which we repeat like parrots; and it has become quite natural for us to do so. We cannot help it. Great souls, who first felt these great ideas in their hearts, created these words; and at that time many understood their meaning. Later on, ignorant people took up those words to play with them, and they made religion a mere play with words and not a thing to be carried into practice. It has become "my father's religion," "our nation's religion," "our country's religion," and so forth. It has become part of patriotism to profess a certain religion; and patriotism is always partial.

To bring harmony into religion must always be difficult. Yet we shall consider this problem of the harmony of religions.

We see that in every religion there are three parts—I mean in every great and recognized religion. First, there is the philosophy, which presents the whole scope of that religion, setting forth its basic principles, its goal, and the means of reaching that goal. The second part is mythology, which is philosophy made concrete. It consists of legends relating to the lives of men or of supernatural beings, and so forth. It is abstract philosophy made concrete through the more or less imaginary lives of men and supernatural beings. The third part is ritual. This is still more concrete and is made up of forms and ceremonies, various physical attitudes, flowers and incense, and many other things that appeal to the senses.

You will find that all recognized religions have these three elements. Some lay more stress on one, some on another.

Let us now take into consideration the first part, philosophy. Is there one universal philosophy? Not yet. Each religion brings out its own doctrines and insists upon them as being the only true ones. And not only does it do that, but it thinks that he who does not believe in them must go to some horrible place. Some will even draw the sword to compel others to believe as they do. This is not through wickedness, but through a particular disease of the human brain, called fanaticism. They are very sincere, these fanatics, the most sincere of human beings; but they are quite as irresponsible as other lunatics in the world. This disease of fanaticism is one of the most dangerous of all diseases. All the wickedness of human nature is roused by it. Anger is stirred up, nerves are strung high, and human beings become like tigers.

Is there any mythological similarity, any mythological harmony, any universal mythology accepted by all religions? Certainly not. All religions have their own mythology; only each of them says, "My stories are not mere myths." . . .

Next come the rituals. One sect has one particular form of rituals and thinks that they are holy whereas the rituals of another sect are simply arrant superstition. If one sect worships a peculiar sort of symbol, another sect says, "Oh, it is horrible." Take for instance a common Hindu symbol: the phallus. This is certainly a sex symbol; but gradually that aspect of it has been forgotten, and it stands now as a symbol of the Creator. Those Hindus who use this as their symbol never connect it with sex; to them it is just a symbol, and there it ends. But a man from another race or creed sees in it nothing but the phallus, and condemns it; yet at the same time he may be doing something which to the so-called phallus-worshippers appears most horrible. Let me take two cases for illustration: the phallus symbol and the sacrament of the Christians. To the Christians the phallus is horrible, and to the Hindus the Christian sacrament is horrible. They say that the Christian sacrament, the killing of a man and the eating of his flesh and the drinking of his blood to get the good qualities of that man, is cannibalism. This is what some of the savage tribes do. If a man is brave, they kill him and eat his heart, because they think that it will give them the qualities of courage and bravery possessed by that man. Even such a devout Christian as Sir John Lubbock admits this and says that the origin of this Christian symbol is in this primitive idea. Most Christians, of course, do not admit this view of its origin, and what it originally implied never comes to their minds. It stands for a holy thing, and that is all they care about. So even in rituals there is no universal symbol which can command general recognition and acceptance. . . .

What, then, do I mean by the ideal of a universal religion? I do not mean any one universal philosophy or any one universal mythology or any one universal ritual held alike by all; for I know that this world must go on working, wheel within wheel, this intricate mass of machinery, most complex, most wonderful. What can we do then? We can make it run smoothly, we can lessen the friction, we can grease the wheels, as it were. How? By recognizing the natural necessity of variation. Just as we have recognized unity as our very nature, so we must also recognize variation. We must learn that truth may be expressed in a hundred thousand ways, and that each of these ways is true as far as it goes. We must learn that the same thing can be viewed from a hundred different standpoints and yet be the same thing. Take for instance the sun. Suppose a man standing on the earth looks at the sun when it rises in the morning; he sees a big ball. Suppose he starts on a journey towards the sun and takes a camera with him, taking photographs at every stage of his journey until he reaches the sun. The photographs of each stage will be seen to be different from those of the other stages; in fact, when he gets back, he brings with him so many photographs of so many different suns, as it would appear; and yet we know that the same sun was photographed by the man at the different stages of his progress.

Even so is it with the Lord. Through high philosophy or low, through the most exalted mythology or the grossest, through the most refined ritualism or arrant fetishism, every sect, every soul, every nation, every religion, consciously or unconsciously is struggling upward toward God; every vision of truth that man has is a vision of Him and of none else. Suppose we all go with vessels in our hands to fetch water from a lake. One has a cup, another a jar, another a bucket, and so forth, and we all fill our vessels. The water in each case naturally takes the form of the vessel carried by each of us. He who brought the cup has the water in the form of a cup; he who brought the jar—his water takes the shape of a jar;

and so forth. But in every case, water, and nothing but water, is in the vessel. So it is with religion. Our minds are like these vessels, and each one of us is trying to arrive at the realization of God. God is like that water filling these different vessels, and in each vessel the vision of God takes the form of the vessel. Yet He is One. He is God in every case. This is the only recognition of universality that we can get. . . .

What I want to propagate is a religion that will be equally acceptable to all minds. It must be equally philosophic, equally emotional, equally mystical, and equally conducive to action. If professors from the colleges come—or scientific men and philosophers—they will court reason. Let them have it as much as they want. There will be a point beyond which they will discover they cannot go without breaking with reason. If they say, "These ideas of God and salvation are superstitions; give them up," I shall reply: "Mr. Philosopher, this body of yours is a bigger superstition. Give *it* up. Don't go home to dinner or to your philosophic chair. Give up the body, and if you cannot, cry quarter and sit down." Religion must be able to show us how to realize the knowledge that teaches that this world is one, that there is but one Existence in the universe. Similarly, if the mystic comes, we must welcome him, be ready to teach him the science of mental analysis, and practically demonstrate it before him. If emotional people come, we must sit with them and laugh and weep in the name of the Lord; we must "drink the cup of love and become mad." And if the energetic worker comes, we must work with him with all the energy that we have. And this combination will be the ideal, the nearest approach to a universal religion.[1]

From *Practical Vedanta: I*

Vedanta preaches the ideal, and the ideal, as we know, is always far ahead of the real, of the practical, as we may call it. There are two tendencies in human nature: one to reconcile the ideal with life and the other to elevate life to the ideal. It is a great thing to understand this; for we are often tempted by the former. I think that I can do a certain kind of work. Most of it, perhaps, is bad; most of it, perhaps, has a motive power of passion behind it—anger, or greed, or selfishness. Now, if any man comes to preach to me a certain ideal, the first step towards which is to give up selfishness, to give up self-enjoyment, I think that that is impractical. But when a man brings an ideal which can be reconciled with my selfishness, I am glad and at once jump at it. That is the ideal for me. As the word *orthodox* has been manipulated into various forms, so has the word *practical*. "My doxy is orthodoxy; your doxy is heterodoxy." So with practicality. What I think is practical is to me the only practicality in the world. If I am a shopkeeper, I think shopkeeping the only practical pursuit in the world. If I am a thief, I think stealing is the best means of being practical; others are not practical. You see how we all use this word *practical* for things that *we* like and can do. Therefore I ask you to understand that Vedanta, though it is intensely practical, is always so in the sense of the ideal. It does not preach an impossible ideal, however high it may be, and it is high enough for an ideal.

In one word, this ideal is that you are divine. "Thou art That." This is the essence of Vedanta. After all its ramifications and intellectual gymnastics, you know the human soul to be pure and omniscient; you see that such superstitions as birth and death are entire nonsense when spoken of in connexion with the soul. The soul was never born and will never die, and all these ideas that we are going to die and are afraid to die are mere superstitions. And all such ideas as that we can do this, or cannot do that, are superstitions. We can do everything. Vedanta teaches men to have faith in themselves first. As certain religions of the world say that a man who does not believe in a Personal God outside himself is an atheist, so Vedanta says that a man who does not believe in himself is an atheist. Not believing in the glory of our own soul is what Vedanta calls atheism.

To many this is, no doubt, a terrible ideal, and most of us think that this ideal can never be reached; but Vedanta insists that it can be realized by everyone. One may be either man or woman or child; one may belong to any race—nothing will stand as a bar to the realization of this ideal, because, as Vedanta shows, it is realized already, it is already there. All the powers in the universe are already ours. It is we who have put our hands before our eyes and cry that it is dark. Know that there is no darkness around you. Take your hands away and there is the light which was from the beginning. Darkness never existed; weakness never existed. We who are fools cry that we are weak; we who are fools cry that we are impure. Thus Vedanta insists not only that the ideal is practical, but that it has been so always, and that this ideal, this Reality, is our own nature. Everything else that you see is false, untrue. As soon as you say, "I am a little mortal being," you are saying something which is not true, you are giving the lie to yourselves, you are hypnotizing yourselves into something vile and weak and wretched. Vedanta recognizes no sin; it recognizes only error. And the greatest error, it says, is to think that you are weak, that you are a sinner, a miserable creature, and that you have no power and cannot do this or that. Every time you think in that way, you rivet, as is were, one more link in the chain that binds you down, you add one more layer of hypnotism upon your soul. Therefore whosoever thinks he is weak is wrong, whosoever thinks he is impure is wrong, and is throwing a bad thought into the world.

This we must always bear in mind: In Vedanta there is no attempt at reconciling the present life, the hypnotized life, this false life which we have assumed, with the ideal; but this false life must go, and the real life, which has always existed, must manifest itself, must shine out. No man becomes purer and purer; it is a matter of greater manifestation of the perfection that has always been in him. The veil drops away, and the native purity of the soul begins to manifest itself. Everything is ours already—infinite purity, freedom, love, and power. . . .

 . . . Never tell yourselves or others that you are weak. Do good if you can, but do not injure the world. You know in your inmost heart that many of your limited ideas—this humbling of yourself, and praying and weeping to imaginary beings—are superstitions. Tell me one case where these prayers have been answered from outside. All the answers came from your own hearts. You know there are no ghosts, but no sooner are you in the dark than you feel a little creepy sensation. That is because in your childhood you have had all these fearful ideas put into your heads. But do not teach these things to others—through fear of society and public opinion, or for fear of incurring the hatred of friends, or for fear of losing cherished superstitions. Be masters of all these. What is there to be taught in religion more than the oneness of the universe, and faith in oneself? All the efforts of mankind for thousands of years past have been directed towards this one goal, and mankind is yet to work it out. It is your turn now and you already know the truth. For it has been taught on all sides. Not only philosophy and psychology, but the materialistic sciences have declared it. Where is the scientific man today who fears to acknowledge the truth of this oneness of the universe? Who is there who dares talk of many worlds? All these are superstitions.

There is only one Life, one World; and this one Life, this one World, appears to us to be manifold. This manifoldness is like a dream. When you dream, one dream passes away and another comes. None of your dreams are real. The dreams come one after another; scene after scene unfolds before you. So it is in this world of ninety per cent misery and ten per cent happiness. Perhaps after a while it will appear as ninety per cent happiness, and we shall call it heaven. But a time comes to the sage when the whole thing vanishes and this world appears as God Himself, and his own soul as that God. It is not true that there are many worlds; it is not true that there are many lives. All this manifoldness is the manifestation of that One. That One is manifesting Himself as many—as matter, spirit, mind, thought, and everything else. Therefore the first step for us to take is to teach the truth to ourselves and to others. Let the world resound with this ideal and let superstitions vanish. Tell it to men who are weak, and persist in telling it.

"You are the Pure One. Awake and arise, Almighty One! This sleep does not become you. Awake and arise; it does not befit you. Think not that you are weak and miserable. Almighty One, arise and awake, and manifest your true nature. It is not fitting that you think yourself a sinner. It is not fitting that you think yourself weak." Say that to the world, say it to yourselves, and see what a practical result follows; see how with an electric flash the truth is manifested, how everything is changed. Tell it to men and show them their power. Then they will learn how to apply it in their daily lives.[2]

From *Inspired Talks*

In the world, take always the position of the giver. Give everything and look for no return. Give love, give help, give service, give any little thing you can, but *keep out barter*. Make no conditions and none will be imposed. Let us give out of our own bounty, just as God gives to us.

The Lord is the only Giver, all the world are only shopkeepers. Get His cheque and it must be honored everywhere.

"God is the inexplicable, inexpressible essence of love," to be known, but never defined.

Obey the Scriptures until you are strong enough to do without them, then go beyond them. Books are not an end-all. Verification is the only proof of religious truth. Each must verify for himself; and no teacher who says "I have seen, but *you* cannot" is to be trusted, only that one who says "you can see too." All Scriptures, all truths are Vedas, in all times, in all countries; because these truths are to be *seen* and any one may discover them.

"When the sun of Love begins to break on the horizon, we want to give up all our actions unto God and when we forget Him for a moment, it grieves us greatly."

Let nothing stand between God and your love for him. Love Him, love Him, love Him, and let the world say what it will. Love is of three sorts—one demands, but gives nothing; the second is exchange, and the third is love without thought of return, love like that of the moths for the light.

"Love is higher than works, than *Yoga,* than knowledge."

Work is merely a schooling for the doer, it can do no good to others. We must work out our own problem, the prophets only show us how to work. *"What you think, you become,"* so if you throw your burden on Jesus, you will have to think of Him and thus become like Him, you *love* Him. Extreme love and highest knowledge are one.

Desire nothing; think of God and look for no return; it is the desireless who bring results. The begging monks carry religion to every man's door; but they think that they do nothing, they claim nothing, their work is unconsciously done. If they should eat of the tree of knowledge, they would become egoists and all the good they do would fly away. As soon as we say "I" we are humbugged all the time, and we call it "knowledge," but it is only going round and round like a bullock tied to a tree. The Lord has hidden Himself best and His work is best; so he who hides himself best, accomplishes most. Conquer *yourself* and the whole universe is yours.

Seek truth for truth's sake alone, look not for bliss. It may come, but do not let that be your incentive. Have no motive except God. Dare to come to Truth even through hell.

The more we grow in love and virtue and holiness, the more we see love and virtue and holiness outside. All condemnation of others really condemns ourselves. Adjust the microcosm, which is in your power to do, and the macrocosm will adjust itself for you. It is like the hydrostatic paradox, one drop of water can balance the universe. We cannot see outside what we are not inside. The universe is to us what the huge engine is to the miniature engine; an indication of any error in the tiny engine leads us to imagine trouble in the huge one.

Every step that has been really gained in the world has been gained by love; criticising can never do any good, it has been tried for thousands of years. Condemnation accomplishes nothing.

The universe is ours to enjoy, but want nothing. To want is weakness. Want makes us beggars and we are sons of the king, not beggars.

So long as the "skin sky" surrounds man, that is, so long as he identifies himself with his body, he cannot see God.

Everything we know is a compound and all sense-knowledge comes through analysis. To think that mind is a simple, single or independent, is dualism. Philosophy is not got by studying books; the more you read books, the more muddled becomes the mind. The idea of unthinking philosophers was that the mind was a simple, and this led them to believe in free-will. Psychology, the analysis of the mind, shows the mind to be a compound, and every compound must be held together by some outside force; so the will is bound by the combination of outside forces. Man cannot even will to eat unless he is hungry. Will is subject to desire. But we are free; everyone feels it.

Everything in the universe is struggling to complete a circle, to return to its source, to return to its only real Source, *Atman*. The search for happiness is a struggle to find the balance, to restore the equilibrium. Morality is the struggle of the bound will to get free and is the proof that we have come from perfection.

The greatest sin is to think yourself weak. No one is greater; realize you are *Brahman*. Nothing has power except what you give it. We are beyond the sun, the stars, the universe. Teach the Godhood of man. Deny evil, create none. Stand up and say, I am the master, the master of all. We forge the chain and we alone can break it.

No action can give you freedom; only knowledge can make you free. Knowledge is irresistible; the mind cannot take it or reject it. When it comes, the mind has to accept it; so it is not a work of the mind, only, its expression comes in the mind.

Work or worship is to bring you back to your own nature. It is an entire illusion that the Self is the body; so even while living here in the body, we can be free. The body has nothing in common with the Self. Illusion is taking the real for the unreal—not "nothing at all."[3]

From *A Letter to the Hale Sisters*

. . . Let your souls ascend day and night like an "unbroken string" unto the feet of the Beloved whose throne is in your own hearts and let the rest take care of themselves, that is the body and everything else. Life is evanescent, a fleeting dream; youth and beauty fade. Say day and night, "Thou art my father, my mother, my husband, my love, my lord, my God—I want nothing but Thee, nothing but Thee, nothing but Thee. Thou in me, I in Thee, I am Thee. Thou art me." Wealth goes, beauty vanishes, life flies, powers fly—but the Lord abideth for ever, love abideth for ever. If there is glory in keeping the machine in good trim, it is more glorious to withhold the soul from suffering with the body—that is the only demonstration of your being "not matter," by letting the matter alone.

Stick to God! Who cares what comes to the body or to anything else! Through the terrors of evil, say—my God, my love!

Through the pangs of death, say—my God, my love! Through all the evils under the sun, say—my God, my love. Thou art here, I see Thee. Thou art with me, I feel Thee. I am Thine, take me. I am not of the world's but Thine, leave not then me. Do not go for glass beads leaving the mine of diamonds! This life is a great chance. What, seekest thou the pleasures of the world!—He is the fountain of all bliss. Seek for the highest, aim at that highest and you *shall* reach the highest.[4]

The Meaning of Religion

Do not depend on doctrines, do not depend on dogmas, or sects, or churches, or temples; they count for little compared with the essence of existence in man, which is divine; and the more this divinity is developed in a man, the more powerful is he for good. Earn that spirituality first, acquire that, and criticize no one, for all doctrines and creeds have some good in them. Show by your lives that religion does not mean words, or names, or sects, but that it means spiritual realization. Only those can understand who have perceived the Reality. Only those who have attained to spirituality can communicate it to others, can be great teachers of mankind. They alone are the powers of light.[5]

NOTES

1. From *The Yogas and Other Works,* Swami Nikhilananda, editor (1953), pp. 387-394.
2. From *Jnana Yoga,* revised edition (1955), pp. 211-213; 221-224.
3. From *Inspired Talks, My Master and Other Writings* (1939).
4. From *Letters of Swami Vivekananda* (1964), pp. 157-158.
5. From *Complete Works of Swami Vivekananda,* Vol. IV (1962), p. 187.

25. Swami Brahmananda

Swami Brahmananda (1863-1922) never attained the world re-known of his brother-disciple, Swami Vivekananda, but those who came in contact with him immediately knew themselves to be in the presence of a great spiritual soul. Though his method of instruction was different, its result was equally effective. Brahmananda was born Rakhal Chandra Ghosh in a village near Calcutta, and first met Sri Ramakrishna when he was a high school student. Ramakrishna immediately recognized Rakhal as a young man of remarkable spirituality, and in a short time they had formed an intimate and indissoluble relationship.

As he grew into manhood, Brahmananda's regal bearing and quiet strength impressed all who met him. When Vivekananda was absent, the brother monks of the Order deferred to Brahmananda in matters of policy and spiritual instruction. He became known as Raja ("king") to them.

Swami Brahmananda served as the first president of the Rama-krishna Order until his death—a period of more than twenty years. During this time, he also assumed the role of spiritual ad-viser and *guru* to a growing number of devotees.

The Eternal Companion is a record of some of his teachings to monks of the Order. They are both practical and inspiring.

Swami Brahmananda

From *The Eternal Companion*

Maharaj*

Doubts will come until you have realized God; therefore you must hold fast to God and pray. Think to yourself: "God *is!* but because

---

* Swami Brahmananda was called "Maharaj" by both his disciples and acquaintances as a title of respect as well as affection. Junior monks of the Ramakrishna Order in India generally refer to their seniors by this name.

of the impurities of my mind I cannot see him. When my heart and mind have become purified, then, through his grace, I shall surely see him!"

God cannot be known by the finite mind. He is beyond the mind and far beyond the intellect. This apparent universe is a creation of the mind. The mind has conjured it up; it is its author, and the mind cannot go beyond its own domain.

Behind this mind of ours there is a subtle, spiritual mind, existing in seed-form. Through the practice of contemplation, prayer, and japam, this mind is developed, and with this development a new vision opens up, and the aspirant realizes many spiritual truths. This, however, is not the final experience. The subtle mind leads the aspirant nearer to God, but it cannot reach God, the supreme Atman. Having reached this stage, the world no longer holds any charm for the aspirant; he becomes absorbed in the consciousness of God. This absorption leads to samadhi, an experience which cannot be described. It is beyond *is* and *is not*. There, there is neither happiness nor misery, neither light nor darkness. All is Infinite Being—inexpressible.

Disciple

Maharaj, how should we perform our worldly duties?

Maharaj

Do your duties conscientiously and without attachment. Always remember that you are only an instrument in the hands of God, and that God himself is the only doer. Keep your mind fixed in God. It is not always easy to keep the mind steady in God while working; the ego creeps in. But never be discouraged by your failures. Repeated failure is inevitable in the beginning, but keep your faith and redouble your efforts. Try hard to live up to your ideal.

Let your watchword be: "I must realize God in this very life!" After all, what is the use of this body and this mind if they do not help you to realize God? Do or die! What does it matter even if you die in the attempt!

Disciple

Maharaj, I have been practicing spiritual disciplines, but as yet I have acquired no taste for them. What shall I do?

Maharaj

The taste for spiritual life cannot be had all at once. No! One has to struggle hard for it. All our energies must be concentrated toward that one achievement; they must not be wasted in any other direction. Onward, onward! Never be satisfied with your present state of growth. Try to create a burning dissatisfaction within yourself. Ask yourself, "What progress am I making? None!" and apply yourself ever more diligently to the task. Sri Ramakrishna used to cry out at the close of each day: "O Mother, another day has gone, and I have not seen you!"

Every night before you go to sleep, think for a while how much time you have spent in doing good deeds and how much time you have wasted; how much time you have spent in meditation and how much you have wasted in idleness. Make your mind strong through the observance of continence and the practice of meditation.

A rich man employs a porter whose duty it is to see that neither thieves, nor cows, nor sheep, nor any other intruder enter the compound. Man's mind is his porter, and the stronger the mind becomes, the better. The mind has also been likened to a restive horse. Such a horse may carry its rider along the wrong path, and only he who can hold the reins and check the horse can keep to the right path.

Struggle on! Do you think that everything is achieved merely by wearing the gerrua cloth [ochre-coloured cloth of the *sannyasin* or monk], or by the renunciation of hearth and home? What spiritual experiences have you had? Time is flying. Waste no more time, for, at most you have only another three or four years in which to struggle intensively. After that your body and mind will grow weak and infirm and your efforts will be limited. What can be achieved without diligence?

You may think: "Let us have yearning, faith, and devotion

first, then we shall begin our spiritual practices." But is that possible? Can we see the day before the break of dawn? When the Lord comes, love, devotion, and faith follow him as his retinue.

Nothing can be achieved without spiritual discipline. Have you not seen what severe disciplines even the *Avataras* underwent? Has anything been gained without labour? What tremendous austerities were practiced by Buddha, Shankara, and others! What burning renunciation!

Real faith cannot be had at the beginning. First realization, then faith. At first the spiritual aspirant must pin his faith—blind faith, it may be—in the words of his guru or some great soul; only then can he advance toward the goal.

Do you know Sri Ramakrishna's parable of the oyster? The oyster floats about on the surface of the water with its shell wide open, waiting for a little drop of the Svati-rain [the rain which falls when the star Svati or Arcturus is in the ascendant]. As soon as it gets the raindrop it dives down to the bottom of the sea and there forms a fine pearl. You, like the oyster, have received the raindrop; you have the grace of your guru; now dive deep into the ocean of bliss and form the pearl—let God be revealed.

Be self-reliant. Self-effort is absolutely necessary to success in the spiritual life. Follow some spiritual discipline for at least three years, and then, if you find you have made no tangible progress, you may come back and slap my face! . . .

How blessed is this human birth! Man alone can find God. To realize him must be man's only purpose. Strive hard to reach him and be free in this very life. . . .

Never be calculating. Is self-surrender possible in a day? When that is achieved everything is achieved. One must struggle hard for it. Existence is eternal. The span of man's life is at most a hundred years. Give up the pleasures of these hundred years if you want to enjoy eternal life and, with it, eternal bliss.

Disciple

Maharaj, how may one control the mind?

Maharaj

Through gradual practice, the mind has to be concentrated upon

God. Keep a sharp eye on the mind and see that no undesirable thoughts or distractions enter in. Whenever they try to crowd in, turn the mind toward God and pray earnestly. Through such practice the mind is brought under control and becomes purified.

When you can feel and know that you are helpless and alone, that you have no other refuge but God; when you feel that you have nothing in life to look forward to, then only will devotion to God arise in you.

Practice japam unceasingly. Practice it with every breath. Practice it until it becomes your second nature; then you will find yourself chanting the name of God as you fall asleep, and again as you awaken.

Know for certain that God can be reached—that his spiritual form can be seen, and that it is possible to talk to him.

Practice these spiritual disciplines, and as you practice, new visions will open up—wonderful, beautiful visions. You may see many aspects of God, and many spiritual forms. Or you may see an ocean of light, or a steady flame. There is no end to this God-unfoldment, this knowledge of infinite Existence, infinite Bliss. Light, light, more light! Therefore, engage yourself in these practices. With great earnestness chant his name and dive deep.

Learn to acquire love and sympathy toward all. Overlook the faults of others. If you cannot help an evil man to become good, of what use is your spiritual life?

Learn patience. Anger is controlled through patience. Be patient, forbearing, and humble. Humility is a great aid in the building of character. Sri Ramakrishna used to say, "He who can forbear, lives. He who cannot, is lost." Again he would say, "Water accumulates on low ground; when the ground is high, it runs off." In a humble man sweetness of character and other good qualities develop naturally.

Try to remember God constantly—even while you are working. In the beginning it is a little difficult, but through practice it becomes easy. Never give up struggling. Too many rules and regulations for spiritual life are no good. The main thing is sincerity and earnestness. If these qualities are in your prayer it will surely reach the Lord. God looks into the heart and not into the words of a man.

People talk of enjoying this world, but what do they know of enjoyment? First become a god and then enjoy. Before that, all so-called enjoyments are the enjoyments of a brute.

If your mind has become pure and you live with pure thoughts, no evil can touch you.

Disciple

Maharaj, there is the song, "I want to taste sugar but not to become sugar." Should that be the attitude of a devotee?

Maharaj

"I want to taste sugar but not become sugar," is for the man who has not yet tasted sugar. When a devotee begins to taste the sweetness of God, he will desire to achieve oneness with him.

Disciple

Are dreams about enlightened men or Divine Incarnations real?

Maharaj

Yes, they are real. Dreams about enlightened souls, gods and goddesses, and Divine Incarnations, are real experiences. They are actual visitations. Many spiritual truths are revealed to one in dreams. The effect and impression of such dreams remain. But one must not speak of them to anybody.

*　　　*　　　*

Disciple

Maharaj, I have tried in various ways to control my senses but I have not succeeded. How can I do this?

Maharaj

If you merely say: "I will conquer lust, I will conquer anger and greed," you can never conquer them; but if you can fix your mind on God, the passions will leave you of themselves. Sri Ramakrishna used to say, "The more you move eastward, the further you are from the west." Call on God, and pray to him. Then the objects of sense will no longer attract you.

Your way of practicing japam and meditation is very superficial.

If you practice casually, devoting only one or two hours a day to meditation, you cannot find God. Lose yourself day and night in his contemplation, in singing his praises and glory; only then will you be blessed with his vision. Dive deep, my children, dive deep. Do not waste your time.

In the primary stage, the aspirant should slowly but steadily increase his hours of meditation. Otherwise, if, because of a momentary enthusiasm, he suddenly tries to increase his hours of meditation, he will find the reaction difficult to bear. He will become depressed, and then he will lose the power to meditate. It is a difficult task to lift a depressed mind and turn it back to spiritual practices.

God's grace is supreme; without it nothing is achieved. Pray to him unceasingly for his grace. Prayer is efficacious. He lovingly hears your prayers.

Hold on for a little while. Do not give your mind up to objects of desire. You must exercise great self-control in everything. Objects of desire! They will follow you like slaves. Then, through his grace, you will find you have no desire for them—nor will you feel any attachment to them.

You have embraced the monastic life, renouncing everything. It does not become you to try to exercise authority over others. That brings great bondage. Whatever you do, know that it is the Lord's work you are doing. Look upon everything and everybody as belonging to Sri Ramakrishna. "Being deluded by egotism, man thinks himself to be the doer."

To tell a lie is the greatest sin. A drunkard or a man who frequents houses of ill fame may be trusted, but never a liar! It is the blackest of sins.

Never find fault or criticize others. Such a habit is harmful to yourself. By thinking continually of the evil in others, the evil will impress itself upon your own mind and the good that is in you will be overshadowed.

Play with God, sing his glory, enjoy the fun! Why should you criticize others? Associate with everybody freely. Be happy with them. Do not indulge in gossip. Only a wicked-hearted man busies himself finding fault with others.

Keep yourself pure and go forward, following your own ideal. Learn to see the good in others. If a man has some goodness, exaggerate his goodness in your mind. Give honor to all, praise all. Do this and sympathy for others will grow. He himself is honored who honors all beings.

Never run down a fellow-man or slight him. Everyone sees the fault in others. Give him your love, make him your own and help him to overcome his weaknesses. A man is composed of both good and evil. It is easy to see the evil in others but a holy man is he who can overlook their evil qualities and help them to become pure and holy.

Remember, my children, you are holy men. You must always be calm, gentle, modest, and kindly of speech. Goodness and purity must flow through every word you utter, every action you perform, through all your behaviour and movements.

I bless you, my children, that whosoever associates with you will find peace of heart. The sleeping God will awaken within them.

What is chastity? Always be truthful. Be self-controlled. Watch your speech. Envy no one. Hate no one. Be jealous of no one. If one practices chastity for twelve years, he attains the highest. You must practice continence.

It is wise to go occasionally to places of pilgrimage and live there for some time. The holy atmosphere and change of scenery are aids to the health of the body and mind. These places are also conducive to meditation.

The heart must be purified. This world is full of pitfalls. Effort must be your motto if you want to grow spiritually. Keep watch over every small desire which arises and control it. Strengthen the will and everything else will be simple.

*   *   *

Devotee

Please tell me how to meditate.

Maharaj

Meditate upon God within the shrine of your heart, or visualize him present before you. Worship him mentally. Just as the ritualistic worshipper offers flowers, and waves incense and lights before the deity in the temple, so should you offer all the articles of worship mentally to the living presence enshrined within your heart. Do not waste any more time. Begin this very day. Practice japam and meditation once in the morning and once in the evening for at least two years. You will find great joy; spiritual emotions will arise; a new vision will open up. You are sure to find some result in two years. Some succeed even in a year. Stick to it! After a while you will find such joy that you will have no inclination to leave your meditation. Get yourself a new seat and use it only for your meditation. Sit straight, keep the right hand over the left, with the palms up. Hold your hands near the center of your body in the region of the heart.

Read sacred scriptures. When you sit down to meditate, do not begin the practice immediately. For a few minutes, banish all alien thoughts and make the mind blank. Then start your meditation. For the first two years, the struggle is hard; afterwards it becomes easy.

If a day comes when you have a lot of work to do, you may meditate only once, or you may finish in ten or fifteen minutes. If the pressure of work is very great, fix your mind on God for a moment, then bow down to him and close your meditation. You can do this in exceptional cases, but not always.

Before meditation wash your hands and face. Observe the two following rules of moral conduct: speak the truth and look upon all women as incarnations of the Divine Mother. If you do these two things, you will find all other moral rules easy to follow.

Devote yourself to God. God *is*. Do not doubt his existence. I am telling you, my child, God *is*. Know for certain that he is.[1]

NOTE

1. From Swami Prabhavananda, *The Eternal Companion* (1947).

26. Rabindranath Tagore

Rabindranath Tagore (1861-1941) has been called the embodiment of all that is best in Indian culture. A prolific writer, Tagore treated in a wide collection of poems, stories, plays, novels, and essays the various periods of Indian history from the Vedic age to the modern, interwoven with his own humanistic and idealistic conceptions of life.

Tagore was born in Calcutta, the youngest member of an illustrious family. His father was Devendranath Tagore, a man of wealth, education, and spiritual discrimination. Rabindranath was sent to England in 1877 to study law, but soon returned to India where he began writing for Bengali periodicals. In 1901, he founded Santiniketan, an unconventional educational institution in which he attempted to promulgate some of his idealistic conceptions. His fame became international in 1913 when he received the Nobel Prize for literature, primarily for his great poetical work *Gitanjali*. Tagore accepted a knighthood in 1915, but resigned it four years later as a protest against the methods employed by the British to put down disturbances in the Punjab.

Tagore was particularly concerned with social reforms, which he considered even more important than political changes—though at the time India was bristling under British rule. "Tagore," as one writer expressed it, ". . . was the incarnation of the spirit of toleration and fellowship." Tagore was convinced that India's priceless spiritual wisdom belonged to the world, not merely to her own people. This wisdom he attempted to convey to the world through his writings. In them, of course, we also see reflected Tagore the man, with his love of simplicity, of children, and profound belief in an all-pervasive Divine Consciousness.

Gitanjali is perhaps the most mystical of his writings. As a lover of beauty and of life, Tagore sought to express his devotion in the language of the poet—at the same time recognizing the Divine

Source of his inspiration. "This little flute of a reed," he writes of himself, "thou hast carried over hills and dales, and hast breathed through it melodies eternally new."

Rabindranath Tagore

From *Gitanjali*

1

Thou hast made me endless, such is thy pleasure. This frail vessel thou emptiest again and again, and fillest it ever with fresh life.

This little flute of a reed thou hast carried over hills and dales, and hast breathed through it melodies eternally new.

At the immortal touch of thy hands my little heart loses its limits in joy and gives birth to utterance ineffable.

Thy infinite gifts come to me only on these very small hands of mine. Ages pass, and still thou pourest, and still there is room to fill.

2

When thou commandest me to sing it seems that my heart would break with pride; and I look to thy face, and tears come to my eyes.

All that is harsh and dissonant in my life melts into one sweet harmony—and my adoration spreads wings like a glad bird on its flight across the sea.

I know thou takest pleasure in my singing. I know that only as a singer I come before thy presence.

I touch by the edge of the far spreading wing of my song thy feet which I could never aspire to reach.

Drunk with the joy of singing I forget myself and call thee friend who art my lord.

23

Art thou abroad on this stormy night on thy journey of love, my friend? The sky groans like one in despair.

I have no sleep to-night. Ever and again I open my door and look out on the darkness, my friend!

I can see nothing before me. I wonder where lies thy path!

By what dim shore of the ink-black river, by what far edge of the frowning forest, through what mazy depth of gloom art thou threading thy course to come to me, my friend?

29

He whom I enclose with my name is weeping in this dungeon. I am ever busy building this wall all around; and as this wall goes up into the sky day by day I lose sight of my true being in its dark shadow.

I take pride in this great wall, and I plaster it with dust and sand lest a least hole should be left in this name; and for all the care I take I lose sight of my true being.

36

This is my prayer to thee, my lord—strike, strike at the root of penury in my heart.

Give me the strength lightly to bear my joys and sorrows.

Give me the strength to make my love fruitful in service.

Give me the strength never to disown the poor or bend my knees before insolent might.

Give me the strength to raise my mind high above daily trifles.

And give me the strength to surrender my strength to thy will with love.

50

I had gone a-begging from door to door in the village path, when thy golden chariot appeared in the distance like a gorgeous dream and I wondered who was this King of all kings!

My hopes rose high and methought my evil days were at an end, and I stood waiting for alms to be given unasked and for wealth scattered on all sides in the dust.

The chariot stopped where I stood. Thy glance fell on me and thou camest down with a smile. I felt that the luck of my life had come at last. Then of a sudden thou didst hold out thy right hand and say "What hast thou to give to me?"

Ah, what a kingly jest was it to open thy palm to a beggar to beg! I was confused and stood undecided, and then from my wallet I slowly took out the least little grain of corn and gave it to thee.

But how great my surprise when at the day's end I emptied my bag on the floor to find a least little grain of gold among the poor heap. I bitterly wept and wished that I had had the heart to give thee my all.

53

Beautiful is thy wristlet, decked with stars and cunningly wrought in myriad-coloured jewels. But more beautiful to me thy sword with its curve of lightning like the outspread wings of the divine bird of Vishnu, perfectly poised in the angry red light of the sunset.

It quivers like the one last response of life in ecstasy of pain at the final stroke of death; it shines like the pure flame of being, burning up earthly sense with one fierce flash.

Beautiful is thy wristlet, decked with starry gems; but thy sword, O lord of thunder, is wrought with uttermost beauty, terrible to behold or to think of.

72

He it is, the innermost one, who awakens my being with his deep hidden touches.

He it is who puts his enchantment upon these eyes and joyfully plays on the chords of my heart in varied cadence of pleasure and pain.

He it is who weaves the web of this *maya* in evanescent hues of gold and silver, blue and green, and lets peep out through the folds his feet, at whose touch I forget myself.

Days come and ages pass, and it is ever he who moves my heart in many a name, in many a guise, in many a rapture of joy and of sorrow.

76

Day after day, O lord of my life, shall I stand before thee face to face? With folded hands, O lord of all worlds, shall I stand before thee face to face?

Under thy great sky in solitude and silence, with humble heart shall I stand before thee face to face?

In this laborious world of thine, tumultuous with toil and with struggle, among hurrying crowds shall I stand before thee face to face?

And when my work shall be done in this world, O King of kings, alone and speechless shall I stand before thee face to face?

82

Time is endless in thy hands, my lord. There is none to count thy minutes.

Days and nights pass and ages bloom and fade like flowers. Thou knowest how to wait.

Thy centuries follow each other perfecting a small wild flower.

We have no time to lose, and having no time we must scramble for our chances. We are too poor to be late.

And thus it is that time goes by while I give it to every querulous man who claims it, and thine altar is empty of all offerings to the last.

At the end of the day I hasten in fear lest thy gate be shut; but I find that yet there is time.

83

Mother, I shall weave a chain of pearls for thy neck with my tears of sorrow.

The stars have wrought their anklets of light to deck thy feet, but mine will hang upon thy breast.

Wealth and fame come from thee and it is for thee to give or to withhold them. But this my sorrow is absolutely mine own, and when I bring it to thee as my offering thou rewardest me with thy grace.

100

I dive down into the depth of the ocean of forms, hoping to gain the perfect pearl of the formless.

No more sailing from harbour to harbour with this my weather-beaten boat. The days are long passed when my sport was to be tossed on waves.

And now I am eager to die into the deathless.

Into the audience hall by the fathomless abyss where swells up the music of toneless strings I shall take this harp of my life.

I shall tune it to the notes of for ever, and, when it has sobbed out its last utterance, lay down my silent harp at the feet of the silent.

103

In one salutation to thee, my God, let all my senses spread out and touch this world at thy feet.

Like a rain-cloud of July hung low with its burden of unshed showers let all my mind bend down at thy door in one salutation to thee.

Let all my songs gather together their diverse strains into a single current and flow to a sea of silence in one salutation to thee.

Like a flock of homesick cranes flying night and day back to their mountain nests let all my life take its voyage to its eternal home in one salutation to thee.[1]

The Realization of the Infinite

The Upanishads say: "Man becomes true if in this life he can apprehend God; if not, it is the greatest calamity for him." [*Kena*]

But what is the nature of this attainment of God? It is quite evident that the infinite is not like one object among many, to be definitely classified and kept among our possessions, to be used as an ally specially favouring us in our politics, warfare, money-making, or in social competitions. We cannot put our God in the same list with our summer-houses, motor-cars, or our credit at the bank, as so many people seem to want to do.

We must try to understand the true character of the desire that a man has when his soul longs for his God. Does it consist of his wish to make an addition, however valuable, to his belongings? Emphatically no! It is an endlessly wearisome task, this continual adding to our stores. In fact, when the soul seeks God she seeks her final escape from this incessant gathering and heaping and never coming to an end. It is not an additional object that she seeks, but it is the *nityo nityanam,* the permanent in all that is impermanent, the *rasanam rasatamah,* the highest abiding joy unifying all enjoyments. Therefore when the Upanishads teach us to realize everything in Brahma [Brahman], it is not to seek something extra, not to manufacture something new.

Know everything that there is in the universe as enveloped by God. Enjoy whatever is given by him and harbour not in your mind the greed for wealth which is not your own.   [*Isha Upanishad*]

When you know that whatever there is is filled by him and whatever you have is his gift, then you realize the infinite in the finite, and the giver in the gifts. Then you know that all the facts of the reality have their only meaning in the manifestation of the one truth, and all your possessions have their only significance for you, not in themselves but in the relation they establish with the infinite.

So it cannot be said that we can find Brahma [Brahman] as we find other objects; there is no question of searching for him in one thing in preference to another, in one place instead of somewhere else. We do not have to run to the grocer's shop for our morning light; we open our eyes and there it is; so we need only give ourselves up to find that Brahma is everywhere. . . .

We see everywhere in the history of man that the spirit of renunciation is the deepest reality of the human soul. When the soul says of anything, "I do not want it, for I am above it," she gives utterance to the highest truth that is in her. When a girl's life outgrows her doll, when she realises that in every respect she is more than her doll is, then she throws it away. By the very act of possession we know that we are greater than the things we possess. It is a perfect misery to be kept bound up with things lesser than ourselves. This it is that Maitreyi felt when her husband gave her his property on the eve of leaving home. She asked him, "Would these material things help one to attain the highest?"—or, in other words, "Are they more than my soul to me?" When her husband answered, "They will make you rich in worldly possessions," she said at once, "Then what am I to do with these?" It is only when a man truly realises what his possessions are that he has no more illusions about them; then he knows his soul is far above these things and he becomes free from their bondage. Thus man truly realises his soul by outgrowing his possessions, and man's progress in the path of eternal life is through a series of renunciations.

That we cannot absolutely possess the infinite being is not a mere intellectual proposition. It has to be experienced, and this experience is bliss. The bird, while taking its flight in the sky, experiences at every beat of its wings that the sky is boundless, that its wings can never carry it beyond. Therein lies its joy. In the cage the sky is limited; it may be quite enough for all the purposes of the bird's life, only it is not more than is necessary. The bird cannot rejoice within the limits of the necessary. It must feel that what it has is immeasurably more than it ever can want or comprehend, and then only can it be glad.

Thus our soul must soar in the infinite, and she must feel every moment that in the sense of not being able to come to the end of her attainment is her supreme joy, her final freedom.[2]

NOTES

1. From *Gitanjali* (Song Offerings) (1913).
2. From *Sadhana—The Realization of Life* (1913).

27. Mahatma Gandhi

Mohandas Gandhi (1869-1948) is regarded by the world today as India's greatest political figure and, certainly during his lifetime, was revered as a man of saintliness by millions of poverty-stricken Indian villagers. "Reactionary or revolutionary," Nehru said of Gandhi, "he has changed the face of India, given pride and character to a cringing and demoralized people, built up strength and consciousness in the masses, and made the Indian problem a world problem."

Though Gandhi felt compassion for the poor throughout his life, he himself came from a wealthy and influential family. After an early marriage, Gandhi left India to study law in England. He became a barrister in 1891, and then settled in Johannesburg, South Africa, to practice law. However, Gandhi soon began to involve himself in the problems at home, and it was during these years he developed his ideas of *satyagraha* or the resistance of injustice by noncooperation. Much of his thinking in this direction was influenced by his reading of Ruskin, Thoreau, the *Bhagavad-Gita,* and the New Testament. It was also during this period that he undertook a vow of chastity, and later poverty.

Gandhi returned to India in 1914, and rapidly gained recognition as the leading voice in the struggle for Indian independence. He was jailed a number of times for his subversive activities, but as he said of this later, "I always get the best bargains from behind Indian bars." Gandhi advocated, in the strongest terms, a revival of home industries, particularly cloth weaving, for which he was sharply criticized by India's progressives. But the villagers took to it with enthusiasm. The Mahatma ("Great Soul"), as he was popularly known, was particularly famous for his extended fasts, which he employed as means to still rebellion and exact political concessions.

There is no question that Gandhi, despite his contradictory and unpredictable nature, was one of the significant forces in India's history. His tremendous appeal undoubtedly stemmed from his capacity to feel compassion for the people of India, and his willingness to speak not simply as a sage, but live a life of austerity and renunciation as well. Although he drew upon Western ideas for his inspiration, he still harked back to the Indian spiritual doctrines of truth and of an underlying order connecting man and the universe.

Gandhi believed quite strongly that the practice of *brahmacharya* (see selection) or continence was one of the important steps toward making India a strong nation. Although it was an idealistic hope, it is a concept which is greatly respected, particularly in the East, by those who seek to live a higher life.

Mahatma Gandhi

Chastity

What . . . is *Brahmacharya* [chastity]? It means that men and women should refrain from carnal knowledge of each other. That is to say, they should not touch each other with a carnal thought, they should not think of it even in their dreams. Their mutual glances should be free from all suggestion of carnality. The hidden strength that God has given us should be conserved by rigid self-discipline, and transmitted into energy and power—not merely of body, but also of mind and soul.

But what is the spectacle that we actually see around us? Men and women, old and young, without exception, are caught in the meshes of sensuality. Blinded for the most part by lust, they lose all sense of right and wrong. I have myself seen even boys and girls behaving as if they were mad under its fatal influence. I too have behaved likewise under similar influences, and it could not well be otherwise. For the sake of a momentary pleasure, we sacrifice in an instant all the stock of vital energy that we have laboriously accumulated. The infatuation over, we find ourselves in a miserable condition. The next morning we feel hopelessly weak and tired, and the mind refuses to do its work. . . .

. . . The older we grow the keener should our intellect be; the longer we live the greater should be our capacity to communicate the benefit of our accumulated experience to our fellow men. And such is indeed the case with those who have been true Brahmacharis. They know no fear of death, and they do not forget God even in the hour of death; nor do they indulge in vain desires. They die with a smile on their lips, and boldly face the day of judgment. They are true men and women; and of them alone can it be said that they have conserved their health.

We hardly realize the fact that incontinence is the root cause of most vanity, anger, fear and jealousy in the world. If our mind is not under our control, if we behave once or oftener every day more foolishly than even little children, what sins may we not commit consciously or unconsciously? How can we pause to think of the consequences of our actions, however vile or sinful they may be?

But you may ask, "Who has ever seen a true Brahmachari in this sense? If all men should turn Brahmacharis, would not humanity be extinct and the whole world go to rack and ruin?" We will leave aside the religious aspect of this question and discuss it simply from the secular point of view. To my mind, these questions only betray our timidity and worse. We have not the strength of will to observe Brahmacharya, and therefore set about finding pretexts for evading our duty. The race of true Brahmacharis is by no means extinct; but if they were commonly to be met with, of what value would Brahmacharya be? Thousands of hardy labourers have to go and dig deep into the bowels of the earth in search for diamonds, and at length they get perhaps merely a handful of them out of heaps and heaps of rock. How much greater, then, should be the labour involved in the discovery of the infinitely more precious diamond of a Brahmachari? If the observance of Brahmacharya should mean the end of the world, that is none of our business. Are we God that we should be so anxious about its future? He who created it will surely see to its preservation. We need not trouble to inquire whether other people practice Brahmacharya or not. When we enter a trade or profession, do we ever pause to consider what the fate of the world would be if all men were to do likewise? The true Brahmachari will, in the long run, discover for himself answers to such questions.

But how can men engrossed in the cares of the material world put these ideas into practice? What about those who are married? What shall they do who have children? And what shall be done by those people who cannot control themselves? We have already seen what is the highest state for us to attain. We should keep this ideal constantly before us, and try to approach it to the utmost of our capacity. When little children are taught to write the letters of the alphabet, we show them the perfect shapes of the letters, and they try to reproduce them as best they can. In the same way, if we steadily work up to the ideal of Brahmacharya we may ultimately succeed in realizing it. What if we have married already? The law of Nature is that Brahmacharya may be broken only when the husband and wife feel a desire for progeny. Those, who, remembering this law, violate Brahmacharya once in four or five years, will not become slaves to lust, nor lose much of their stock of vital energy. . . .

We are, in this respect far worse than even the lower animals; for in their case the male and the female are brought together solely with the object of breeding from them. Man and woman should regard it a sacred duty to keep apart from the moment of conception up to the time when the child is weaned. But we go on with our fatal merry-making blissfully forgetful of that sacred obligation. This almost incurable disease enfeebles our mind and leads us to an early grave, after making us drag a miserable existence for a short while. Married people should understand the true function of marriage, and should not violate Brahmacharya except with a view to progeny.

But this is so difficult under our present conditions of life. Our diet, our ways of life, our common talk, and our environments are all equally calculated to rouse animal passions; and sensuality is like a poison eating into our vitals. Some people may doubt the possibility of our being able to free ourselves from this bondage. This . . . is written not for those who go about with such doubting of heart, but only for those who are really in earnest, and who have the courage to take active steps for self-improvement. . . .

. . . The true laws of health demand that the man who loses his wife, as well as the woman that loses her husband, should remain single ever after. There is a difference of opinion among medical men as to whether young men and women need ever let their vital energy escape, some answering the question in the affirmative, others in the negative. But while doctors thus disagree we must not give way to over-indulgence from an idea that we are supported by medical authority. I can affirm, without the slightest hesitation, from my own experience as well as that of others, that sexual enjoyment is not only not necessary for, but is positively injurious to health. All the strength of body and mind that has taken long to acquire is lost all at once by a single dissipation of the vital energy. It takes a long time to regain this lost vitality, and even then there is no saying that it can be thoroughly recovered. A broken mirror may be mended and made to do its work, but it can never be anything but a broken mirror.

As has already been pointed out, the preservation of our vitality is impossible without pure air, pure water, pure and wholesome food, as well as pure thoughts. So vital indeed is the relation between health and morals that we can never be perfectly healthy unless we lead a clean life. The earnest man, who, forgetting the errors of the past, begins to live a life of purity, will be able to reap the fruit of it straightaway. Those who practice true Brahmacharya even for a short period will see how their body and mind improve steadily in strength and power, and they will not at any cost be willing to part with this treasure. I have myself been guilty of lapses even after having fully understood the value of Brahmacharya, and have of course paid dearly for it. I am filled with shame and remorse when I think of the terrible contrast between my condition before and after these lapses. But from the errors of the past I have now learnt to preserve this treasure intact, and I fully hope, with God's grace to continue to preserve it in the future; for I have, in my own person, experienced the inestimable benefits of Brahmacharya. I was married early, and had become the father of children as a mere youth. When, at length, I awoke to the reality of my situation, I found that I was steeped in ignorance about the fundamental laws of our being. I shall consider myself amply rewarded for writing this chapter if at least a single reader takes a warning from my failings and experiences, and profits thereby. Many people have told—and I also believe it—that I am full of energy and enthusiasm, and that I am by no means weak in mind; some even accuse me of strength bordering on obstinacy. Nevertheless there is still bodily and mental ill-health as a legacy of the past. And yet when compared with my friends, I may call myself healthy and strong. If even after twenty years of sensual enjoyment, I have been able to reach this state, how much better off should I have been if I had kept myself pure during those twenty years as well? It is my full conviction, that if only I had lived a life of unbroken Brahmacharya all through, my energy and enthusiasm would have been a thousandfold greater and I should have been able to devote them all to the furtherance of my country's cause as my own. If an imperfect Brahmachari like myself can reap such benefit, how much more wonderful must be the gain in power—physical, mental, as well as moral—that unbroken Brahmacharya can bring to us. . . .

No one need despair. My Mahatmaship is worthless. It is due to my outward activities, due to my politics which is the least part of me and is therefore evanescent. What is of abiding worth is my insistence on truth, nonviolence and Brahmacharya, which is the real part of me. That permanent part of me, however, small, is not to be despised. It is my all. I prize even the failures and disillusionments which are but steps towards success.[1]

[“Self-Restraint v. Self-Indulgence”]

Selected Passages

A humble person is not himself conscious of his humility. Truth and the like perhaps admit of measurement, but not humility. Inborn humility can never remain hidden, and yet the possessor is unaware of its existence. The story of Vasishtha and Vishvamitra* furnishes a very good case in point. Humility should make the possessor realize that he is as nothing. Directly one imagines oneself to be something, there is egotism. If a man who keeps observances is proud of keeping them, they will lose much, if not all of their values. And a man who is proud of his virtue often

* Two ancient sages whose lives are recounted in *The Ramayana*.

becomes a curse to society. Society will not appreciate it, and he himself will fail to reap any benefit out of it. Only a little thought will suffice to convince us, that all creatures are nothing more than a mere atom in this universe. Our existence as embodied beings is purely momentary; what are a hundred years in eternity? But if we shatter the chains of egotism, and are melted in the ocean of humanity, we share its dignity. To feel that we are something is to set up a barrier between God and ourselves. To cease feeling that we are something is to become one with God. A drop in the ocean partakes of the greatness of its parent, although it is unconscious of it. But it is dried up, as soon as it enters upon an existence independent of the ocean. We do not exaggerate when we say that life is a mere bubble.

A life of service must be one of humility. One, who would sacrifice his life for others, has hardly time to reserve for himself a place in the sun. Inertia must not be mistaken for humility, as it has been in Hinduism. True humility means most strenuous and constant endeavour entirely directed to the service of humanity. God is performing continuous action without resting for a single moment. If we would serve Him or become one with Him, our activity must be as unwearied as His. There may be rest in store for the drop which is separated from the ocean, but not for the drop in the ocean, which knows no rest. The same is the case with ourselves. As soon as we become one with the ocean in the shape of God, there is no more rest for us, nor indeed do we need rest any longer. Our very sleep is action. For we sleep with the thought of God in our hearts. This restlessness constitutes true rest. This never-ceasing agitation holds the key to peace ineffable. This supreme state of total surrender is difficult to describe, but not beyond the bounds of human experience.[2]

["The Gita and Satyagraha"]

God is that indefinable something which we all feel but which we do not know. To me God is Truth and Love, God is ethics and morality. God is fearlessness, God is the source of light and life and yet He is above and beyond all these. God is conscience. He is even the atheism of the atheist. He transcends speech and reason. He is personal God to those who need His touch. He is the purest essence. He simply Is to those who have faith. He is long suffering. He is patient but He is also terrible. He is the greatest democrat the world knows. He is the greatest tyrant ever known. We are *not,* He alone *Is.*[3]

[*Young India,* March 5, 1925]

I do not regard God as a person. Truth for me is God, and God's Law and God are not different things or facts, in the sense that an earthly king and his law are different. Because God is an Idea, Law Himself. Therefore, it is impossible to conceive God as breaking the Law. He, therefore, does not rule our actions and withdraw Himself. When we say He rules our actions, we are simply using human language and we try to limit Him. Otherwise, He and His Law abide everywhere and govern everything. Therefore, I do not think that He answers in every detail every request of ours, but there is no doubt that He rules our action and I literally believe that not a blade of grass grows or moves without His will.

[*Harijan,* March 23, 1940]

You cannot realize the wider consciousness, unless you subordinate completely reason and intellect, and the body too.

[*Harijan,* date unrecorded]

But He is no God who merely satisfies the intellect, if He ever does. God to be God must rule the heart and transform it. He must express Himself in every smallest act of His votary. This can only be done through a definite realization more real than the five senses can ever produce. Sense perceptions can be, often are, false and deceptive, however real they may appear to us. Where there is realization outside the senses it is infallible. It is proved not by extraneous evidence but in the transformed conduct and character of those who have felt the real presence of God within. Such testimony is to be found in the experiences of an unbroken line of prophets and sages in all countries and climes. To reject this evidence is to deny oneself.

[*Young India,* October 11, 1928]

I am a man of peace. I believe in peace. But I do not want

peace at any price. I do not want the peace you find in stone; I I do not want the peace that you find in the grave; but I do want the peace which you find embedded in the human breast which is exposed to the arrows of a whole world, but which is protected from all harm by the Power of the Almighty God.

[*Young India,* January 19, 1922]

NOTES

1. From Ronald Duncan, editor, *Selected Writings of Mahatma Gandhi* (1951), pp. 159-165.
2. Ibid., pp. 52-53
3. This and the following passages from Kshitis Ray, editor, *Gandhi Memorial Peace Issue.*

28. Sri Aurobindo

Sri Aurobindo (1872-1950) is primarily known for his revolutionary metaphysical ideas and, in his earlier years, for his political writings and agitations for Indian independence. Aurobindo is unquestionably a brilliant and comprehensive thinker, though his critics have accused him of using the language of Western philosophy to apply to states and conditions of existence related only to his own personal experiences. Nevertheless, his philosophical concepts are highly unusual, and, in many ways, profound.

Sri Aurobindo's central teaching, which he developed fully in his massive three-volume work *The Life Divine,* is a philosophy of cosmic salvation in which both man and the universe gradually attain the qualities of divinity through a process of evolution. Aurobindo flatly rejects the view held by Shankara and his followers (the orthodox nondualists) that Brahman is the only Reality and the world, being a manifestation of Brahman, is in some sense illusory.

Sri Aurobindo was convinced that Consciousness or Brahman manifests itself as matter through a process of what he called "involution" and then progressively brings about an unfoldment of its powers through evolution. He believed that it is possible, through the use of various techniques, to evolve mind and body into a state of divinity. Thus will be created a divinized community, a heaven on earth. For this to happen, two things are necessary. First, one must prepare oneself by the practice of a new form of yoga ("integral yoga") which permeates physical, social, and cultural life. Second, God must "descend" into human experience.

In 1910, Aurobindo went to Pondicherry and there founded the *ashram* or religious community which bears his name. His writings also include *The Synthesis of Yoga* (1948), *Savitri: a Legend and a Symbol* (1950), and the much respected *Essays on the Gita* (1928).

Sri Aurobindo

From *Essays on the Gita*

. . . a man's way to liberation and perfection lies through an increasing impersonality. It is his ancient and constant experience that the more he opens himself to the impersonal and infinite, to that which is pure and high and one and common in all things and beings . . . the less he is bound by his ego and by the circle of the finite, and the more he feels a sense of largeness, peace, pure happiness. The pleasure, joy, satisfaction which the finite by itself can give or the ego in its own right attain, is transitory, petty and insecure.

To dwell entirely in the ego-sense and its finite conceptions, powers, satisfactions is to find this world for ever full of transience and suffering. The finite life is always troubled by a certain sense of vanity, for this fundamental reason that the finite is not the whole or the highest truth of life; life is not entirely real until it opens into the sense of the infinite. It is for this reason that the Gita opens its gospel of works by insisting on the Brahmic consciousness, the impersonal life, that great object of the discipline of the ancient sages. For the impersonal, the infinite, the One in which all the permanent, mutable, multiple activity of the world finds above itself its base of permanence; security and peace, is the immobile Self . . . the Brahman. If we see this, we shall see that to raise one's consciousness and the poise of one's being out of limited personality into this infinite and impersonal Brahman is the first spiritual necessity. To see all beings in this one Self is the knowledge which raises the soul out of egoistic ignorance and its works and results; to live in it is to acquire peace and firm spiritual foundation.

The way to bring about this great transformation follows a double path; for there is the way of knowledge and there is the way of works, and the Gita combines them in a firm synthesis.* The way of knowledge is to turn the understanding, the intelligent

---

* Jnana yoga and karma yoga, respectively.

will away from its downward absorption in the workings of the mind and the senses, and upward to the Self, the Purusha or Brahman. It is to make it dwell always on the one idea of the one Self and not in the many-branching conceptions of the mind and the many-streaming impulses of desire. Taken by itself this path would seem to lead to the complete renunciation of works, to an immobile passivity and to the severance of the soul from Nature. But in reality such an absolute renunciation, passivity, and severance are impossible. Purusha and Prakriti are twin principles of being which cannot be severed, and so long as we remain in Nature, our workings in Nature must continue, even though they may take a different form or rather a different sense from those of the un-enlightened soul.

The real renunciation—for renunciation, *sannyasa,* there must be—is not the fleeing from works, but the slaying of ego and desire. The way is to abandon attachment to the fruit of works even while doing them, and the way is to recognise Nature as the agent and leave her to do her works and to live in the soul as the witness and sustainer, watching and sustaining her, but not attached either to her actions or their fruits. The ego, the limited and troubled personality is then quieted and merged in the consciousness of the one impersonal Self, while the works of Nature continue to our vision to operate through all these "becomings" or existences which are now seen by us as living and acting and moving, under her impulsion entirely, in this one infinite Being. Our own finite existence is seen and felt to be only one of these and its workings are seen and felt to be those of Nature, not of our real Self—which is the silent impersonal unity. The ego claimed them as its own doings and therefore we thought them ours; but the ego is now dead and henceforth they are no longer ours, but Nature's. We have achieved, by the slaying of ego, impersonality in our being and consciousness; we have achieved, by the renunciation of desire, impersonality in the works of our nature. We are free not only in inaction, but in action; our liberty does not [now] depend on a physical and temperamental immobility and vacancy, nor do we fall from freedom directly we act. Even in a full current of natural action the impersonal soul in us remains calm, still, and free.[1]

From *The Life Divine*

The earliest preoccupation of man in his awakened thoughts and, as it seems, his inevitable and ultimate preoccupation—for it survives the longest periods of scepticism and returns after every banishment—is also the highest which his thought can envisage. It manifests itself in the divination of Godhead, the impulse towards perfection, the search after pure Truth and unmixed Bliss, the sense of a secret immortality. The ancient dawns of human knowledge have left us their witness to this constant aspiration; to-day we see a humanity satiated but not satisfied. . . . The earliest formula of Wisdom promises to be its last—God, Light, Freedom, Immortality.

These persistent ideals of the race are at once the contradiction of its normal experience and the affirmation of higher and deeper experiences which are abnormal to humanity and only to be attained, in their organised entirety, by a revolutionary individual effort or an evolutionary general progression. To know, possess and be the divine being in an animal and egoistic consciousness, to convert our twilight or obscure physical mentality into the plenary supramental illumination, to build peace and a self-existent bliss where there is only a stress of transitory satisfactions besieged by physical pain and emotional suffering, to establish an infinite freedom in a world which presents itself as a group of mechanical necessities, to discover and realise the immortal life in a body subjected to death and constant mutation—this is offered to us as the manifestation of God in Matter and the goal of Nature in her terrestrial evolution. To the ordinary material intellect which takes its present organisation of consciousness for the limit of its possibilities, the direct contradiction of the unrealised ideals with the realised fact is a final argument against their validity. But if we take a more deliberate view of the world's workings, that direct opposition appears rather as part of Nature's profoundest method and the seal of her completest sanction.[2]

From *The Yoga and Its Objects*

God is one but he is not bounded by his unity. We see him here as one who is always manifesting as many, not because he cannot help it, but because he so wills, and outside manifestation he is . . . indefinable, and cannot be described as either one or many. That is what the Upanishads and other sacred books consistently teach; . . . but also and consequently he is "this man, yonder woman, that blue-winged bird, this scarlet-eyed." He is *santa* [finite], he is *ananta* [infinite]. . . . "I am the *asvattha* tree," says Sri Krishna in the Gita, "I am death, I am Agni-Vaishvanara, I am the heat that digests food, I am Vyasa, I am Vasudeva, I am Arjuna." All that is the play of his *chaitanya* in his infinite being, his manifestations, and therefore all are real. Maya means nothing more than the freedom of Brahman from the circumstances through which he expresses himself. He is in no way limited by that which we see or think about him. That is the Maya from which we must escape, the Maya of ignorance which takes things as separately existent and not God, not *chaitanya,* the illimitable for the really limited, the free for the bound.

Do you remember the story of Sri Krishna and the Gopis, how Narada found him differently occupied in each house to which he went, present to each Gopi in a different body, yet always the same Sri Krishna? Apart from the devotional meaning of the story, which you know, it is a good image of his World-*Lila* [Play of the Lord]. He is *sarva* [everyone], each Purusha with his apparently different Prakriti and action is he, and yet at the same time he is the Purushottama who is with Radha, the Para Prakriti, and can withdraw all these into himself when he wills and put them out again when he wills. From one point of view they are one with him, from another one yet different, from yet another always different because they always exist, latent in him or expressed at his pleasure. There is no profit in disputing about these standpoints. Wait until you see God and know yourself and him and then debate and discussion will be unnecessary.

The goal marked out for us is not to speculate about these things, but to experience them. The call upon us is to grow into the image of God, to dwell in him and with him and be a channel of his joy and might and an instrument of his works. Purified from all that is *ashubha,* transfigured in soul by his touch, we have to act in the world as dynamos of that divine electricity and send it thrilling and radiating through mankind, so that wherever one of us stands, hundreds around may become full of this light and force, full of God and full of Ananda.

Churches, Orders, theologies, philosophies have failed to save mankind because they have busied themselves with intellectual creeds, dogmas, rites and institutions . . . as if these could save mankind. . . . [They] have neglected the one thing needful, the power and purification of the soul. We must go back to the one thing needful, take up again Christ's gospel of the purity and perfection of mankind, Mahomed's gospel of perfect submission, self-surrender and servitude to God, Chaitanya's gospel of the perfect love and joy of God in man, Ramakrishna's gospel of the unity of all religions and the divinity of God in man, and, gathering all these streams into one mighty river, one purifying and redeeming Ganges, pour it over the death-in-life of a materialistic humanity . . . so that there may be a resurrection of the soul in mankind and the Satyayuga, for a while, return to the world. Nor is this the whole object of the Lila or the Yoga; the reason for which the Avatars descend is to raise up man again and again, developing in him a higher and ever-higher humanity, a greater and yet greater development of divine being, bringing more and more of heaven again and again upon the earth until our toil is done, our work accomplished and *Sat-chit-ananda* fulfilled in all even here, even in this material universe.

Small is his work, even if he succeeds, who labours for his own salvation or the salvation of a few; infinitely great is his, even if he fail or succeed only partially or for a season, who lives only to bring about peace of soul, joy, purity and perfection among all mankind.[3]

NOTES

1. From *Essays on the Gita* (1950), pp. 115-117.
2. From *The Life Divine*, Vol. I (1939), pp. 1-3.
3. From *The Yoga and Its Objects* (1968), pp. 38-42.

29. Ramana Maharshi

Ramana Maharshi (1879-1950) has gained the attention of the world through his life of ascetic simplicity and through the teaching of a practical means to Self-knowledge. Maharshi lived most of his life on a mountain called Arunchala, a sacred hill near Tiruvannamalai in southern India. It was here that devotees from throughout the world gathered during the latter years of his life, when his fame had spread, to listen to his teachings, ask questions, or simply sit in silence. Maharshi had once said that sages use three methods in which to impart spiritual knowledge: by word, touch, or silence. Although he answered a great many questions verbally, Maharshi quite often resolved doubts and inquiries simply through silence, through the force of his spiritual presence alone.

His early years were typical of most Hindu boys. He liked athletics and the out-of-doors. Then, when he was seventeen, he underwent an intense "death experience" which led to his enlightenment and abandonment of worldly life. In a state of divine absorption, he journeyed to Tiruvannamalai and eventually to the nearby mountain of Arunchala. He remained there for the rest of his life.

The first selection is the Maharshi's own description of his *samadhi,* a state in which he was made vividly aware of the blissful Self yet, as his biographer Arthur Osborne notes, "without impeding the normal perceptions and activities of life." In the final selections Maharshi's method of Self-inquiry as a means to knowledge of the Self is clearly brought out in his interviews with visitors to the *ashram* founded at Tiruvannamalai.

227

Ramana Maharshi

Awakening

"It was about six weeks before I left Madura for good that the great change in my life took place. It was quite sudden. I was sitting alone in a room on the first floor of my uncle's house. I seldom had any sickness, and on that day there was nothing wrong with my health, but a sudden violent fear of death overtook me. There was nothing in my state of health to account for it, and I did not try to account for it or to find out whether there was any reason for the fear. I just felt 'I am going to die' and began thinking what to do about it. It did not occur to me to consult a doctor or my elders or friends; I felt that I had to solve the problem myself, there and then.

"The shock of the fear of death drove my mind inwards and I said to myself mentally, without actually framing the words: 'Now death has come; what does it mean? What is it that is dying? This body dies.' And I at once dramatized the occurrence of death. I lay with my limbs stretched out stiff as though *rigor mortis* had set in and imitated a corpse so as to give greater reality to the enquiry. I held my breath and kept my lips tightly closed so that no sound could escape, so that neither the word 'I' nor any other word could be uttered. 'Well then,' I said to myself, 'this body is dead. It will be carried stiff to the burning ground and there burnt and reduced to ashes. But with the death of this body am I dead? Is the body I? It is silent and inert but I feel the full force of my personality and even the voice of the 'I' within me, apart from it. So I am Spirit transcending the body. The body dies but the Spirit that transcends it cannot be touched by death. That means I am the deathless Spirit.' All this was not dull thought; it flashed through me vividly as living truth which I perceived directly, almost without thought-process. 'I' was something very real, the only real thing about my present state, and all the conscious activity connected with my body was centred on that 'I.' From that moment onwards the 'I' or Self focussed attention on itself by a powerful fascination. Fear of death had vanished once and for all. Absorption in the Self continued unbroken from that time on. Other thoughts might come and go like the various notes of music, but the 'I' continued like the fundamental *sruti* note that underlies and blends with all the other notes.* Whether the body was engaged in talking, reading or anything else, I was still centred on 'I.' Previous to that crisis I had no clear perception of my Self and was not consciously attracted to it. I felt no perceptible or direct interest in it, much less any inclination to dwell permanently in it."[1]

Who Am I?

Sivaprakasam Pillai was one of the intellectuals among the devotees. He had taken philosophy at the university and had already pondered over the mysteries of Being. In 1900 he was appointed to a post in the Revenue Department in South Arcot District. Two years later his work took him to Tiruvannamalai and he heard of the young Swami on the hill. He was captivated at the very first visit. . . .

Pillai

Swami, who am I? And how is salvation to be attained?

Maharshi

By incessant inward enquiry "Who am I?" you will know yourself and thereby attain salvation.

Pillai

Who am I?

Maharshi

The real I or Self is not the body, nor any of the five senses, nor the sense-objects, nor the organs of action, nor the *prana* (breath

---

* The monotone persisting through a Hindu piece of music, like the thread on which beads are strung, represents the Self persisting through all the forms of being.

or vital force), nor the mind, nor even the deep sleep state where there is no cognisance of these.

Pillai

If I am none of these what else am I?

Maharshi

After rejecting each of these and saying "this I am not," that which alone remains is the "I," and that is Consciousness.

Pillai

What is the nature of that Consciousness?

Maharshi

It is *Sat-Chit-Ananda* (Being-Consciousness-Bliss) in which there is not even the slightest trace of the I-thought. This is also called *Mouna* (Silence) or *Atma* (Self). That is the only thing that is. If the trinity of world, ego and God are considered as separate entities they are mere illusions like the appearance of silver in mother of pearl. God, ego and world are really *Sivaswarupa* (the Form of Siva) or *Atmaswarupa* (the form of the Spirit).

Pillai

How are we to realize that Real?

Maharshi

When the things seen disappear the true nature of the seer or subject appears.

Pillai

Is it not possible to realize That while still seeing external things?

Maharshi

No, because the seer and the seen are like the rope and the appearance of a serpent therein. Until you get rid of the appearance of a serpent you cannot see that what exists is only the rope.

Pillai

When will external objects vanish?

Maharshi

If the mind, which is the cause of all thoughts and activities, vanishes, external objects will also vanish.

Pillai

What is the nature of the mind?

Maharshi

The mind is only thoughts. It is a form of energy. It manifests itself as the world. When the mind sinks into the Self then the Self is realized; when the mind issues forth the world appears and the Self is not realized.

Pillai

How will the mind vanish?

Maharshi

Only through the enquiry "who am I?" Though this enquiry also is a mental operation, it destroys all mental operations, including itself, just as the stick with which the funeral pyre is stirred is itself reduced to ashes after the pyre and corpses have been burnt. Only then comes Realization of the Self. The I-thought is destroyed, breath and the other signs of vitality subside. The ego and the *prana* . . . have a common source. Whatever you do, do without egoism, that is without the feeling "I am doing this." When a man reaches that state even his own wife will appear to him as the Universal Mother. True Bhakti . . . is surrender of the ego to the Self. . . .

Pillai

How long should one go on with this enquiry?

Maharshi

As long as there is the least trace of impulses in your mind to cause thoughts. So long as the enemy occupy a citadel they will keep on making sorties. If you kill each one as he comes out, the citadel will fall to you in the end. Similarly, each time a thought rears its head crush it with this enquiry. To crush out all thoughts at their source is called *vairagya* (dispassion). So *vichara* (Self-enquiry) continues to be necessary until the Self is realized. What is required is continuous and uninterrupted remembrance of the Self.

Pillai

Is not this world and what takes place therein the result of God's will? And if so why should God will thus?

Maharshi

God has no purpose. He is not bound by any action. The world's activities cannot affect Him. Take the analogy of the sun. The sun rises without desire, purpose or effort, but as soon as it rises numerous activities take place on earth: the lens placed in its rays produces fire in its focus, the lotus bud opens, water evaporates, and every living creature enters upon activity, maintains it, and finally drops it. But the sun is not affected by any such activity, as it merely acts according to its nature, by fixed laws, without any purpose, and is only a witness. So it is with God. Or take the analogy of space or ether. Earth, water, fire and air are all in it and have their modifications in it, yet none of these affects ether or space. It is the same with God. God has no desire or purpose in His acts of creation, maintenance, destruction, withdrawal and salvation to which beings are subjected. As the beings reap the fruit of their actions in accordance with His laws, the responsibility is theirs, not God's. God is not bound by any actions.[2]

God Looks after Everything

[*The Maharshi received a middle-aged visitor from Andhra.*]

Visitor

A man is said to be divine. Why then does he have regrets?

Maharshi

Divinity refers to the essential nature. The regrets are of *Prakriti*.

Visitor

How is one to overcome regrets?

Maharshi

By realizing the Divinity in himself.

Visitor

How?

Maharshi

By practice.

Visitor

What kind of practice?

Maharshi

Meditation.

Visitor

[My] mind is not steady while meditating.

Maharshi

It will be all right by practice.

Visitor

How is the mind to be steadied?

Maharshi

By strengthening it.

Visitor

How to strengthen it?

Maharshi

It grows strong by *satsanga* (the company of the wise).

Visitor

Shall we add prayers, etc.?

Maharshi

Yes.

Visitor

What of the one who has no regrets?

Maharshi

He is an accomplished Yogi. There is no question about him.

Visitor

People cite disasters, *e.g.,* earthquakes, famines, etc., to disprove God. How shall we meet their contention?

Maharshi

Wherefrom have they come—those who argue [in this way]?

Visitor

They say, "Nature."

Maharshi

Some call it "Nature"—others "God."

Visitor

Are we to keep anything against a rainy day: or to live a precarious life for spiritual attainments?

Maharshi

God looks after everything.

Steadiness of Mind

[*A group of persons were visiting Maharshi.*]

Visitor

How can I keep my mind aright?

Maharshi

A refractory bull is lured to the stall by means of grass. Similarly the mind must be lured by good thoughts.

Visitor

But it does not remain steady.

Maharshi

The bull accustomed to stray takes delight in going astray. However he must be lured with luscious grass to the stall. Even so he will continue to trespass into the neighbours' fields. He must gradually be made to realize that the same kind of good grass can be had in his own place. After a time he will remain in the stall without straying. Later a time will come when, even if driven out of the stall, he will return to the stall without going into the neighbouring fields. So also the mind must be trained to take to right ways. It will gradually grow accustomed to good ways and will not return to wrong ways.

Visitor

What are the good ways to be shown to the mind?

Maharshi

Thought of God.[3]

NOTES

1. From Arthur Osborne, *Ramana Maharshi and the Path of Self-Knowledge.* (1970), pp. 18-19.
   2. Ibid., pp. 85-88.
   3. These two selections from *Talks with Sri Ramana Maharshi,* 4th ed. (1968), pp. 342-343; 352.

Bibliography

AIYAR, V. V. S., translator. *The Kural or the Maxims of Tiruvalluvar.* Tiruchirapalli, South India: Dr. V. V. S. Krishnamurthy, 1952.

ALLCHIN, F. R., translator. *Tulsi Das: The Petition to Ram* (a translation of *Vinaya-patrika*). London: George Allen and Unwin, 1966.

AUROBINDO, SRI. *Essays on the Gita.* New York: Sri Aurobindo Library, 1950.

———. *The Life Divine* in 3 volumes, Vol. I. Calcutta: Arya Publishing House, 1939.

———. *The Yoga and Its Objects.* Pondicherry: Sri Aurobindo Ashram, 1968, paperback.

BEHARI, BANKEY. *Minstrels of God,* Parts I & II. Bombay: Bharatiya Vidya Bhavan, 1956, paperback.

BÜHLER, GEORG, translator. *The Laws of Manu.* New York: Dover Publications, Inc. 1969, paperback.

DUNCAN, RONALD, editor. *Selected Writings of Mahatma Gandhi.* London: Faber & Faber, 1951.

ISHERWOOD, CHRISTOPHER. *Ramakrishna and His Disciples.* New York: Simon and Schuster, 1965; 1970, paperback.

———, editor. *Vedanta for the Western World.* Hollywood: Vedanta Press, 1961. New York: Viking Press, 1969, paperback.

MAHARSHI, SRI RAMANA. *Talks with Sri Ramana Maharshi.,* 4th ed. Tiruvannamalai: Sri Ramanasramam, 1968.

NIKHILANANDA, SWAMI, translator. *The Gospel of Sri Ramakrishna.* New York: Ramakrishna Vivekananda Center, 1942.

NITYASWARUPANANDA, SWAMI, translator. *Ashtavakra Samhita.* Calcutta: Advaita Ashrama, 1969.

OSBORNE, ARTHUR. *Ramana Maharshi and the Path of Self-Knowledge.* New York: Samuel Weiser, Inc. 1970, paperback.

PANDIT, M. P. *Gems from the Tantras (Kularnava) (First Series).* Madras: Ganesh & Co., 1969.

PRABHAVANANDA, SWAMI. *The Eternal Companion.* Hollywood: Vedanta Press, 1947. New enlarged edition, Hollywood: Vedanta Press, 1970, hard and paperback.

————, with the assistance of Frederick Manchester. *The Spiritual Heritage of India.* New York: Doubleday, 1964. Hollywood: Vedanta Press, 1969, paperback.

————, translator. *Srimad Bhagavatam: The Wisdom of God.* New York: G. P. Putnam's Sons, 1943. New York: Capricorn Books, 1968, paperback.

————, translator and commentator. *The Way of Divine Love as Taught by Narada.* (Unpublished material.)

———— and ISHERWOOD, CHRISTOPHER, translators. *The Song of God: Bhagavad-Gita.* Hollywood: Vedanta Press, 1951. New York: New American Library, 1951, paperback.

———— and ————, translators and commentators. *How to Know God: The Yoga Aphorisms of Patanjali.* Hollywood: Vedanta Press, 1966. New York: New American Library, 1969, paperback.

———— and ————, translators. *Shankara's Crest-Jewel of Discrimination.* Hollywood: Vedanta Press, 1947. New York: New American Library, 1970, paperback.

———— and JOHNSON, CLIVE, editors. *Prayers and Meditations Compiled from the Scriptures of India.* Hollywood: Vedanta Press, 1967.

———— and MANCHESTER, FREDERICK, translators. *The Upanishads: Breath of the Eternal.* Hollywood: Vedanta Press, 1947. New York: New American Library, 1957, paperback.

RAY, KSHITIS, editor. *Gandhi Memorial Peace Issue.* (Santiniketan: Visva-Bharati Quarterly.) No date given.

SHASTRI, HARI PRASAD, translator. *The Ramayana of Valmiki* in 3 volumes, Vol. I. London: Shanti Sadan, 1957.

TAGORE, RABINDRANATH. *Gitanjali (Song Offerings).* London: Macmillan & Co., 1913. Boston: Bruce Humphries, Inc., paperback.

————, assisted by Evelyn Underhill, translator. *One Hundred Poems of Kabir.* London: Macmillan & Co., Ltd., 1954, Indian edition.

————. *Sadhana—The Realization of Life.* London: Macmillan & Co., 1913.

THIBAUT, GEORGE, translator. *The Vedanta Sutras of Badarayana* in two parts. New York: Dover Publications, Inc., 1962, paperback.

VIVEKANANDA, SWAMI. *Complete Works* in 8 volumes. Calcutta: Advaita Ashrama. Vol. III, 1960; Vol. IV, 1962.

————. *Inspired Talks, My Master and Other Writings.* New York: Ramakrishna Vivekananda Center, 1939.

————. *Jnana Yoga,* revised edition. New York: Ramakrishna Vivekananda Center, 1955.

————. *Letters of Swami Vivekananda.* Calcutta: Advaita Ashrama, 1964.

————. *The Yogas and Other Works* (edited by Swami Nikhilananda). New York: Ramakrishna Vivekananda Center, 1953.

FOR FURTHER READING

BHATTACHARYA, HARIDAS, editor. *The Cultural Heritage of India*, Vols. I-IV. Calcutta: Ramakrishna Mission Institute of Culture, 1958.

HIRIYANNA, M. *Outlines of Indian Philosophy*. Mystic, Conn.: Lawrence Verry, Inc., 1932. London: George Allen and Unwin, 1968, paperback.

ISHERWOOD, CHRISTOPHER. *Essentials of Vedanta*. Hollywood: Vedanta Press, 1969.

————, editor. *Vedanta for Modern Man*. Hollywood: Vedanta Press, 1951. New York: Collier Books, 1962, paperback.

NARAYAN, R. K. *Gods, Demons, and Others*. New York: Viking Press, 1964.

NIKHILANANDA, SWAMI. *Hinduism: Its Meaning for the Liberation of the Spirit*. London: George Allen & Unwin, 1959.

————, translator. *The Upanishads*, Vols. I-IV. New York: Bonanza Books, 1959.

PAVITRANANDA, SWAMI. *Common Sense About Yoga*. Mayavati: Advaita Ashrama, 1967.

PRABHAVANANDA, SWAMI. *Religion in Practice*. Hollywood: Vedanta Press, 1968.

————. *The Sermon on the Mount According to Vedanta*. Hollywood: Vedanta Press, 1964.

RADHAKRISHNAN, S. *Indian Philosophy*, Vols. I & II. London: George Allen & Unwin, Ltd., 1967.

SARADANANDA, SWAMI. *Sri Ramakrishna, the Great Master*. Madras: Sri Ramakrishna Math, 1963.

SMITH, HUSTON. *The Religions of Man*. New York: Harper & Row, 1958; paperback, 1965. (See chapter on Hinduism.)

TAPASYANANDA, SWAMI and NIKHILANANDA, SWAMI. *The Holy Mother: Her Life and Conversations*. Madras: Sri Ramakrishna Math, 1958.

THORNE, SABINA, editor. *Precepts for Perfection: Teachings of the Disciples of Sri Ramakrishna*. Hollywood: Vedanta Press, 1961.

VIRAJANANDA, SWAMI. *Toward the Goal Supreme*. Calcutta: Advaita Ashrama, 1968, paperback.

YALE, JOHN, editor. *What Religion Is in the Words of Swami Vivekananda*. New York: Julian Press, 1962.

YATISWARANANDA, SWAMI. *Adventures in Religious Life*. Madras: Sri Ramakrishna Math, 1962.

Glossary

Advaita (ad vai′ ta)   Nondualistic Vedanta; see *Vedanta*.

ahamkara (a ham kā′ ra)   The ego sense.

akshara (äk sha′ ra)   Unchanging; also a name of Brahman.

ananda (ä′ nan da)   Bliss, joy.

Arjuna (ar′ ju na)   Hero of the *Mahabharata*; friend and disciple of Sri Krishna in the *Bhagavad-Gita*.

asana (ä′ sa na)   Position or posture of the body during meditation; also the place where one sits for meditation.

ashvattha (ash vat′ tha)   The holy fig tree.

Atharva Veda (a tar′ va ve′ da)   See *Vedas*.

Atman (ät′ man)   The Spirit or Self which resides in every creature as the immanent Godhead.

avatar (a va tār′)   A divine Incarnation.

Ayodhya (a yodh′ yä)   The capital of Rama's kingdom in Uttar Pradesh, India.

bhakta (bhak′ ta)   A devotee of God; one who practices *bhakti*.

bhakti yoga (bhak′ ti yo′ ga)   The path of devotion, one of the four main paths to union with God.

Bhishma (bhish′ ma)   One of the great heroes of the *Mahabharata*.

Brahma (brah′ ma)   One of the Hindu Trinity. God, the Creator.

brahmacharya (brah′ ma char′ ya)   Chastity in thought, word, and deed. *Brahmachari*   One who practices *brahmacharya*.

Brahman (brah′ man)   The impersonal absolute existence or transcedent Godhead.

Brahmana (brah′ man a)   See *caste*.

Brahmin (brah′ min)   See *caste*.

buddhi (bud′ dhi)   The discriminative faculty of the mind.

caste   Former social system of India. The four main castes are: *Brahmin* or *Brahmana* or priest caste; *kshatriya* or warrior caste; *vaishya* or merchant caste; *shudra* or servant caste.

Chaitanya (chai′ tan ya)   Spiritually awakened consciousness; also Sri Krishna Chaitanya, great saint and spiritual teacher of India.

chakras (chak' ras)   The seven yogic centers of consciousness.

chitta (chit' ta)   In Yoga terminology, the mind-stuff, whose three components are *manas*, *buddhi*, and *ahamkara*.

darshan (dar' shan)   Paying respects to a holy place or person by a ceremonial visit; also the blessing or purification felt in the presence of holiness; also vision or experience—also philosophy.

dharana (dhä' ra nä)   The practice of concentration, the sixth limb of raja yoga.

dharma (dhar' ma)   Religious duty; also the way of life which a man's nature imposes upon him.

dhyana (dhyä' na)   The practice of meditation or prolonged meditation. The seventh limb of raja yoga.

Gayatri (gä' ya tree)   Sacred Vedic verse recited daily by orthodox Hindus.

Girdhar (gird' har)   A name of Krishna.

Gita (gee' ta).   (Lit. "Song")   A shortened form for the *Bhagavad-Gita* ("Song of God").

gopi (go' pee)   Milkmaid of Brindaban. The gopis were companions and devotees of Sri Krishna.

guna (gu' na)   Any of the three types of energy, *sattva*, *rajas*, and *tamas*, which make up the world of mind and matter.

guru (gu' ru)   A spiritual teacher who assumes responsibility for the spiritual life of his disciple and leads him to salvation.

Hari (ha' ree)   A name of the Lord as Vishnu-Krishna, and as Rama.

japa (ja' pa)   The practice of repeating one of God's names, usually a *mantra*. Also called japam.

Janaka (ja' na ka)   A famous king and saint of ancient India.

jiva (jee' va)   The individual soul or human self. Philosophically it is the *Atman* identified with its coverings of body, mind, and senses.

jnana yoga (gyä' na yo' ga)   The path of knowledge, one of the four main paths to union with the Divine.

jnani (gyä' nee)   A follower of the path of knowledge.

Kali (kä' lee)   A name of the Divine Mother, preserver and destroyer of the world.

Kaliyuga (kä' lee yu' ga)   See *yuga*.

karma (kar' ma)   Action. Also the sum of the consequences of an individual's actions in this and previous lives.

karma yoga (kar' ma yo' ga)   The path of selfless work, one of the four main paths to union with the Divine.

Keshava (ke' sha va)   A name of Krishna.

Krishna (krish' na)   One of the most widely worshiped incarnations of Hinduism. The great spokesman of the *Bhagavad-Gita* and the *Mahabharata.*

kshatriya (kshat' ri ya)   See *caste.*

lila (lee' la)   The divine play of God in His creation; the relative world of space, time, and causation.

lotus (lo' tus)   The ideal of beauty and holiness; a symbol of non-attachment; a figurative representation of the spiritual centers of consciousness in the human body.

Mahabharata (ma hä' bhä' ra ta)   Famous Hindu epic poem in which the *Bhagavad-Gita* is embedded.

M.   Mahendranath Gupta, one of Sri Ramakrishna's foremost householder disciples, author of *The Gospel of Sri Ramakrishna.*

Maitreyi (moi tre' yee)   Wife of the sage Yagnavalkya in the *Brihadaranyaka Upanishad,* a model of spiritual discrimination.

mahatma (ma hat' mä)   A high-souled person.

manas (ma' nas)   A component of the mind which receives sense impressions and presents them to the *buddhi.*

mantra (man' tra)   A sacred formula or name of God, given to a disciple at the time of his initiation by a *guru.* Also, mantram.

maya (mä' yä)   The cosmic illusion on account of which the One appears as many, the Absolute as relative; ignorance obscuring the vision of God.

meditation   Prolonged concentration achieved through repeated practice.

nahabat (na' ha bat)   A music tower or bandstand.

nirvana (nir vä' na)   State of spiritual enlightenment in which the individual ego is absorbed into God.

niyama (nee' ya ma)   In the practice of *yoga,* observance of the virtues of purity, contentment, and devotion.

Om (or Aum)   The sacred syllable representing both the Impersonal and Personal aspects of God; the sound symbol of Brahman.

Pandavas (pän' da vas)   The five princes of the *Mahabharata.*

paramahamsa (pa' ra ma ham' sa)   A monk of the highest type; a supreme knower of Brahman.

prana (prä' na)   The sum total of primal energy from which all mental and physical energy has evolved; the vital breath that sustains life in a physical body.

pranayama (prä nä yä' ma)   Control of the vital energy through the practice of breathing exercises; the fourth limb of *raja yoga.*

pratyahara (prat' yä hä' ra)   In yoga practice, withdrawal of the mind from sense objects; the fifth limb of *raja yoga.*

Puranas (pu rä' nas)   Sacred Hindu scriptures which popularize the philosophical teachings of the Upanishads by means of stories of saints, sages, and kings.

Purusha (pu' ru sha)   The Godhead dwelling within the body; the *Atman.*

rajas (rä' jas)   One of the three *gunas;* the principle of activity or restlessness.

Rama (rä' ma)   One of the divine incarnations of Hinduism; hero of the *Ramayana.*

Ramayana (rä' mä' ya na)   The most ancient Sanskrit epic poem which describes the life of Sri Rama.

Rig Veda (rig' ve' da)   The oldest of the four Vedas. Spelled "Rik" when not followed by the word *Veda.*

sadhana (sä' dha nä)   The practice of spiritual disciplines.

sadhu (sä' dhu)   A holy man, usually a monk.

sahasrara (sa' ha srä' ra)   The highest center of consciousness, located at the top of the head, symbolically spoken of as the thousand-petaled *lotus.*

samadhi (sa mä' dhee)   The superconscious state in which man experiences his identity with the ultimate reality.

samsara (sam sä' ra)   The ceaseless cycle of birth, death, and rebirth to which the individual man is subject as long as he remains ignorant of his identity with *Brahman.*

Sankhya (sängkh' ya)   One of the six systems of orthodox Hindu philosophy.

sannyasi (san yä' see)   A monk who has taken the final vows of renunciation.

Sarada Devi (sä' ra dä de' vee)   The wife of Sri Ramakrishna; also known as the Holy Mother.

Sat-chit-ananda (sat' chit ä nan' da)   Absolute Existence, Consciousness and Bliss; an epithet of *Brahman.*

sattva (sat' va)   One of the three *gunas;* the principle of tranquillity and purity.

Satyagraha (sat' yä gra' ha)   The philosophy of nonviolent, passive resistance.

Self   The *Atman* or inner Godhead; the ego (if not capitalized).

Shaiva (shy' va)   A worshiper of Shiva.

Shakti (shak' tee)   God as Mother of the universe. A worshiper of Shakti is called a *Shakta.*

Shiva (Shi' va)   One of the Hindu Trinity; God, the Dissolver.

Sri or *Shri* (shree)   A term of reverence used before the name of a deity, a holy personality, or a sacred book or place.

shruti (shru' tee)   Scriptural teachings revealed to sages in transcendental consciousness. Considered eternal.

Shukadeva (shu' ka de' va)   Sage of ancient India and narrator of the *Bhagavata Purana.*

Shyama (shyä' mä)   A name of the Divine Mother Kali.

smriti (smri' tee)   Auxiliary scriptures which elaborate and illustrate the *Vedas* or *shruti.*

sudra (shū' dra)   See *caste.*

swami (swä' mi)   A spiritual teacher; a sannyasin or monk.

tamas (ta' mas)   One of the three *gunas,* the principle of inactivity or inertia.

Tantra (tan' tra)   A system of religious philosophy in which the Divine Mother or *Shakti* is worshiped; also the scriptures identified with this worship.

tapas (ta' pas)   Religious austerity or penance.

twice-born   A Hindu who has his second or spiritual birth at the time of his investiture with the sacred thread.

Upanishad (u pan' i shad)   A sacred scripture which forms the philosophical or Knowledge Portion of the *Vedas.*

Vaishnava (vaish' na va)   A devotee of Vishnu.

vaishya (vaish' ya)   See *caste.*

Valmiki (väl' mee kee)   Author of the *Ramayana.*

Varuna (va' ru na)   A Vedic god; presiding deity of the waters.

Vasudeva (vä' su de' va)   A name of Krishna.

Vedanta (ve dän' ta)   A religious philosophy which has evolved from the teachings of the *Vedas;* also one of the six systems of Hindu thought.

Vedas (ve' das)   The oldest scriptures in the world, which serve as the basis for Hindu thought.

Vishnu (vish' nu)   One of the Hindu Trinity; God, the Preserver.

vritti (vrit' ti)   A thought-wave in the mind.

Vyasa (vyä' sa)   Reputed author of the *Mahabharata* and the *Bhagavata.*

Yajur Veda (ya' jur ve' da)   The third of the four *Vedas.*

yama (ya' ma)   In *yoga* practice, ethical behavior.

yoga (yo' ga)   1. Union of the individual soul with the Godhead. 2. The method by which such union is achieved.

yogi (yo' gi)   One who practices *yoga.*

yuga (yu' ga)   According to Hindu mythology, one of four ages into which the duration of a cycle (*kalpa*) of the world's existence is divided. They are the *Satya, Treta, Dwapara,* and *Kali.*